CHASING LOVE

SEAN MCDOWELL

Lifeway Press®
Brentwood, Tennessee

EDITORIAL TEAM | STUDENT MINISTRY PUBLISHING

Ben Trueblood
Director, Student Ministry

Karen Daniel
Editorial Team Leader

Timothy Fox
Writer

Stephanie Cross, Kyle Wiltshire
Content Editors

Amanda Mejias, April-Lyn Caouette
Production Editors

Amy Lyon, Shiloh Stufflebeam
Graphic Designers

Published by Lifeway Press® © 2020 Sean McDowell
Revised 2023

ISBN 978-1-4300-8507-2 • Item 005846044

Dewey decimal classification: 241.66

Subject headings: CHRISTIANITY / CHRISTIAN ETHICS (MORAL THEOLOGY) / SPECIFIC MORAL ISSUES / SEXUAL ETHICS

Unless indicated otherwise, all Scripture quotations are taken from The Holy Bible, English Standard Version, copyright © 2000, 2001 by Crossway Bibles, a division of Good News Publishers. 1996, 2000, 2001, 2002. Used by permission of NavPress. All rights reserved. Represented by Tyndale House Publishers, Inc.

To order additional copies of this resource, write to Lifeway Church Resources Customer Service; 200 Powell Place, Suite 100, Brentwood, TN 37027; order online at www.lifeway.com; phone toll free 800.458.2772; or email orderentry@lifeway.com.

Printed in the United States of America

Student Ministry Publishing • Lifeway Church Resources
200 Powell Place, Suite 100, Brentwood, TN 37027

CONTENTS

ABOUT THE AUTHOR

DR. SEAN MCDOWELL is a gifted communicator with a passion for equipping the church, and in particular young people, to make the case for the Christian faith. He is an Associate Professor in the Christian Apologetics program at Talbot School of Theology in La Mirada, CA.

Sean is one of today's leading apologists. He also teaches a high school Bible class, which helps give him exceptional insight into the prevailing culture. He graduated summa cum laude from Talbot Theological Seminary with a double master's degree in Theology and Philosophy and earned a PhD in Apologetics and Worldview Studies from Southern Baptist Theological Seminary.

Sean is the co-host for the Think Biblically podcast, one of the most popular podcasts on faith and cultural engagement. His YouTube channel (youtube.com/@SeanMcDowell) is one of the top apologetics channels.

Sean is the author, co-author, or editor of over twenty books and Bible studies including *Think Biblically, Evidence that Demands a Verdict* (with Josh McDowell), and *Same-Sex Marriage: A Thoughtful Approach to God's Design for Marriage* (with John Stonestreet). He has one of the leading apologetics blogs, which can be read at seanmcdowell.org.

In April 2000, Sean married his high school sweetheart, Stephanie. They have three children and live in San Juan Capistrano, CA.

INTRODUCTION

This could be one of the most important Bible studies you do at this stage in your life.

I realize this probably sounds a bit melodramatic. Doesn't everyone say that? Well, yes, many do. And I may be guilty of overstatement. But as a father, it comes from my heart.

I can also speak from personal experience. Having been married to my high school sweetheart for over two decades, I am still reaping the benefits of what I learned in similar studies when I was a student. The older I get, the more grateful I am for the people who helped me think biblically about love, sex, and relationships. I hope you have the same experience with this book. If you really take this material to heart, I firmly believe it could be a game-changer for you.

How can you maximize this time? Here are three tips to keep in mind.

MAKE SCRIPTURE YOUR ULTIMATE GUIDE

As you will see, this study is rooted deeply in Scripture. The goal is to understand what the Bible says about sexuality and apply it to our lives. We want to become like the Bereans who examined God's Word every day to see if what Paul said was true (see Acts 17:11). Rather than conforming Scripture to your feelings, thoughts, and desires, I encourage you to commit to doing the opposite: conform your life to what God's Word says.

HAVE AN OPEN MIND

Undoubtedly, something in this study will challenge your thinking; it might even make you uncomfortable. Given the controversial nature of many topics today—especially in the areas of sex, love, and relationships—you may be tempted to immediately dismiss some of these ideas. Don't fall for that trap! Seek to understand first, and be willing to have your mind shaped by God's Word.

SHARE YOUR THOUGHTS WITH OTHERS

One of the best ways to learn something is to share it with other people. The discussion in this study will be helpful, but if you really want it to sink in, talk about it with others. Talk with your parents. Post what you learn on social media. Discuss it with your friends. Be gracious and kind, but share what you learn with the world!

This is going to be fun, and I am honored to go on this journey with you. May God strengthen and guide you as you dive into this book.

Sean

HOW TO USE THIS BOOK

GROUP SESSIONS

This Bible study book includes nine weeks of content. Each week begins with the group session, which uses the following format:

START

This section includes questions and talking points to get the conversation started and to introduce the video segment.

WATCH

This section includes key points from the video teaching with blanks for students to fill in as they watch the video. Videos are available for purchase at lifeway.com/chasinglove or through the Lifeway On Demand app. See page 7 for more details.

DISCUSS

These four pages include questions and statements that guide students to respond to the video teaching and to relevant Bible passages. Since this study covers difficult topics, it's important to consider the age, maturity level, and needs of your group. Consult with church leadership and parents about any controversial questions that may be covered during group time. These are sensitive topics and you might feel uneasy about speaking on them. For more education and information on these topic, please consult Sean McDowell's YouTube channel at youtube.com/@SeanMcDowell.

PERSONAL STUDY

Three days of personal study are provided each week to take students deeper into Scripture and further expand on the biblical truths introduced in the teaching time. These pages challenge students to grow in their understanding of God's Word and to make practical applications to their lives.

HOW TO ACCESS THE VIDEOS

This Bible study has nine videos, one for each session.
These videos enhance the content and help launch discussion.

**TO STREAM THE *CHASING LOVE TEEN BIBLE STUDY* VIDEO
TEACHING SESSIONS, FOLLOW THESE STEPS:**

1. Purchase the group video bundle at lifeway.com/chasinglove.
2. Go to my.lifeway.com/redeem and register or log in to your Lifeway account.
3. Enter the redemption code provided at purchase to gain access to your group-use video license.

Once you've entered your personal redemption code, you can stream the video teaching sessions any time from your Digital Media page on my.lifeway.com or watch them via the Lifeway On Demand app on any mobile device or compatible TV. There's no need to enter your code more than once!

Scan the QR code below to get started.

QUESTIONS? WE HAVE ANSWERS!

Visit support.lifeway.com and search "Video Redemption Code," or call our Tech Support Team at 866.627.8553.

Available in the **Lifeway On Demand** app

Stream on these devices:
ROKU tv firetv

TRUST
GOD

START

What are you chasing in life? Good grades? Success in sports? A high-paying future career? The right boyfriend or girlfriend?

Maybe you care about some—or even all—of these things. But do they capture the depth of what you're really seeking? As good as these things can be, my suspicion is that you want your life to be about something bigger. You want your life to matter.

In this session, we'll learn what it takes to have a meaningful life. We'll discover the essence of what love truly is and how it should drive us to pursue the things that matter the most.

WATCH

WATCH THE SESSION 1 VIDEO. FILL IN THE BLANKS AS YOU FOLLOW ALONG.

1. Will you choose a _____ - _____ life, focused on self-fulfillment, or will you give your life away for a greater cause?

2. Are you living for _____ or an outward love toward _____ and toward other _____?

3. You have a heavenly _____ who _____ you and who wants the best for you.

4. Satan isn't trying to convince you God doesn't _____.

5. Adam and Eve actually don't question the existence of God; they question the _____ of God.

6. Will we believe that God is _____ and that His commandments are for our _____?

7. _____ things are meaningful.

8. God is good, and He actually _____ the best for _____.

9. Who are we going to _____ to?

DISCUSS

READ MATTHEW 6:31–33.

"Therefore do not be anxious, saying, 'What shall we eat?' or 'What shall we drink?' or 'What shall we wear?' For the Gentiles seek after all these things, and your heavenly Father knows that you need them all. But seek first the kingdom of God and his righteousness, and all these things will be added to you."

What are you most anxious about in your life right now?

Write out the promise Jesus gives us if we put His kingdom and righteousness first.

Jesus invites us to embrace a higher calling: to live not for our own pleasure and goals but seek first the things of God. This road is difficult to travel and requires sacrifice, but it's the most meaningful life we can live. How do we begin to seek God's kingdom first?

READ MARK 12:28-31.

And one of the scribes came up and heard them disputing with one another, and seeing that [Jesus] answered them well, asked [Jesus], "Which commandment is the most important of all?" Jesus answered, "The most important is, 'Hear, O Israel: The Lord our God, the Lord is one. And you shall love the Lord your God with all your heart and with all your soul and with all your mind and with all your strength.' The second is this: 'You shall love your neighbor as yourself.' There is no other commandment greater than these."

Simply put, the greatest commandments are to love God and love other people. If we want to seek God's kingdom first, then we must learn how to love God and other people.

But what does it look like to truly love others?

READ 1 JOHN 3:16.

By this we know love, that he laid down his life for us, and we ought to lay down our lives for the brothers.

This doesn't necessarily mean God will literally ask us to lay down our lives (though it might). What it means is that the way to truly love others involves humbling ourselves in obedience to what God has called us to do. Jesus isn't just our model of love; His death on the cross for our sins gives us the ability *to* love. He makes us new creations (see 2 Cor. 5:17)—new people who, by the power of the Holy Spirit who lives inside of us, can give up things the world says we need in order to love God and others well.

What are some real, everyday ways you can lay down your life for others?

The difference between Jesus's invitation and the world's invitation could not be more extreme. The world tells us to *live for* ourselves. Jesus says to *die to* ourselves. The world says to do whatever we want. Jesus says to develop the right wants.

How do we grow those "right wants" in our relationships? How do we seek God and His kingdom in our relationships with other people? Let's focus on what it means to love God and others with our sexuality and in our relationships in this unique cultural moment.

TRUST AND LOVE

One of the most important ingredients of love and relationships is trust.

Whom do you trust most in your life?

Who has the biggest influence on the way you think and act?

How you answer these questions influences every decision you make—and this is especially true in the area of sexuality and relationships. Our world is filled with messages that don't line up with Scripture. And we often find ourselves asking: *Whom should I trust?*

God is a perfect heavenly Father, and He is worthy of our trust. He knows everything, has unlimited power, and loves us more deeply than we can even imagine.

READ ROMANS 5:8.

But God shows his love for us in that while we were still sinners, Christ died for us.

We all have times when we doubt God's love. How can this verse impact those feelings?

Here's the truth: God loves us because of who He is, not because of anything we can do. Jesus didn't require us to repent and believe in Him before He laid down His life for us. He didn't die for good people; He died for sinners. God paid the ultimate price through the death of His Son so we could have eternal life. So, do you trust Him? Do you trust this God?

In the garden of Eden, Satan tempted Adam and Eve by planting seeds of doubt in their confidence in God's character. He caused them to ask: *Does God really have our best interest in mind? Or is He keeping us from something better?*

READ GENESIS 3:6.

So when the woman saw that the tree was good for food, and that it was a delight to the eyes, and that the tree was to be desired to make one wise, she took of its fruit and ate, and she also gave some to her husband who was with her, and he ate.

What three things did Eve notice about the tree and its fruit?

1.

2.

3.

How do these same three things tempt us today?

Adam and Eve ultimately lost confidence in God's goodness and ate the fruit. They doubted His character, and their disobedience brought immeasurable suffering to the world. We're faced with the same kind of choice today.

What are some "fruits" of this world that look pleasurable, fun, and satisfying but are ultimately harmful and sinful?

How does our culture justify these things?

The voices in our culture can be powerful and convincing, especially since we hear them nonstop through social media, school, television, celebrities, and others. Even more challenging, our culture tells us it is loving and right to see these things as good. As a result, we are tempted to stop trusting God and wonder, *Did God really say . . . ?*

If Satan can convince us that God is not good, then we are likely to disregard His commands. However, Scripture teaches us that God is good, and the evidence of Jesus laying down His life for us reveals that He is. We can trust Him and His commands. Not only is God good, but His commands are intended for our good. They are not random or unreasonable. They come directly from who He is and are intended to help us thrive in our lives and relationships.

List some actions and behaviors that you know are truly right or wrong.

How do you know those things are right or wrong?

God is the One who determines what is right and wrong. The world operates according to the laws He created, both physical (such as gravity) and moral (for instance, it's wrong to murder). Physical laws can be observed, but moral laws are written on the human heart. In other words, we can know right and wrong because God has wired people to recognize how He has ordered things, whether they acknowledge it's from Him or not (see Rom. 2:14-16).

It is only when we align our lives with God's design that we can truly be free. Following Jesus helps us align our lives with God's design, and living out Jesus's sexual ethic allows us to thrive.

Why should you trust God and His Word in all things, including love and relationships?

The world says to follow our hearts, to put ourselves first, and to do whatever makes us happy. But many of the things we chase to make us happy will ultimately disappoint and hurt us. Jesus promises us that if we "seek first the kingdom of God and his righteousness," God will grant us true, lasting happiness in Him (see Matt. 6:33).

DAY ONE
GOOD RULES

Write down three words that describe what the world thinks about Christianity and all of its "rules."

Are these words usually positive or negative? Why do you think this is the case?

What are some biblical commands you sometimes find difficult to follow or understand?

Let's see what the Bible says about God's rules.

READ DEUTERONOMY 10:12-13.

"And now, Israel, what does the Lord your God require of you, but to fear the Lord your God, to walk in all his ways, to love him, to serve the Lord your God with all your heart and with all your soul, and to keep the commandments and statutes of the Lord, which I am commanding you today for your good?"

List the three things Israel was commanded to do to show appropriate fear (honor or respect) to God:

1.

2.

3.

Why should we follow God's commands?

Deuteronomy 10:12-13 explain that God's commands are for our own good. Has anyone ever told you that before? As tough as it is to believe sometimes, rules do exist for our own good. Think about your favorite sport. What would it be like if there were no rules, if the players just ran around the field or court doing whatever they wanted—with no boundaries or no fouls? The game wouldn't be a game anymore—it would be chaos. The rules of a game make the sport what it is; rules are what make a game actually playable.

Now let's take this one step further. Think about society.

What would it be like if society had no government or laws?

Would you feel more or less safe in a society without rules?

With no laws, people could steal or hurt others without consequences. People would literally get away with murder. As harsh as they may sometimes seem, rules ultimately exist to protect us.

The same goes for God's laws. He knows what will help society and individuals thrive. For example, let's look at three of the Ten Commandments (see Ex. 20):

- Do not lie.
- Do not steal.
- Do not murder.

Imagine what society would be like if everyone followed just those three rules.

Isn't it possible that God knows what is best for us concerning every other command He has given us, especially when it comes to love and sex?

Has this devotion changed the way you see God's commandments? If so, how?

What is one step you can take to show God you trust that He knows best?

DAY TWO

THE REAL MESSAGE

List some ideas about love and sex that are prevalent in our society today.

Society is filled with messages about love and sex that are contrary to what Christianity teaches. *Is sexual activity really that big of a deal? Does porn really hurt anyone? As long as sex is consensual, there's nothing wrong with it, right? Are you really going to judge someone else for who they love? Why embrace a view of sex, love, and gender that seems so closed-minded? Isn't the Christian sexual ethic unrealistic today anyway?*

Be honest. Do you agree with any of these ideas? If so, why?

These messages contain many of the themes being championed in our society today: tolerance, equality, diversity, and inclusion. Generally, these are all good things. As Christians, we believe all human beings have equal and intrinsic worth and that everyone should be treated with dignity and respect, regardless of their beliefs or lifestyle. But this does not mean we have to affirm everyone's choices and actions.

Let's look at one of the most common messages in our culture and see what the Bible says about it.

Are you really going to judge someone else for how they love?

The world has adopted the notion that it is wrong to judge people for any of their life choices, especially when it comes to sexual behavior. Many are quick to point out that even Jesus says "Judge not" (Matt. 7:1). But there's more to the story.

READ MATTHEW 7:1-5.

"Judge not, that you be not judged. For with the judgment you pronounce you will be judged, and with the measure you use it will be measured to you.

Why do you see the speck that is in your brother's eye, but do not notice the log that is in your own eye? Or how can you say to your brother, 'Let me take the speck out of your eye,' when there is the log in your own eye? You hypocrite, first take the log out of your own eye, and then you will see clearly to take the speck out of your brother's eye."

What are the specific reasons Jesus says not to judge?

Before we can "remove the speck" from others' eyes, what must we do?

Far too many people read the first three words of this passage and stop, thinking it teaches us to never judge anyone. But as we can see, this is not the point at all. This passage teaches us how to judge *the right way*. These words affirm that people do have specks (sins) in their eyes, and it is evident that these specks need to be removed. But if we are struggling with those same sins, we can't go around "fixing" others until we have address them in our own lives. *That* is the point of the passage.

Jesus offers another clarification on proper judgment in John 7:24.

"Do not judge by appearances, but judge with right judgment."

What are some examples of judging only by outward appearances?

What do you think the phrase "right judgment" means?

God's Word is our final standard for right and wrong—not our friends, not celebrities, and not culture. The Bible definitely has things to say about love and sex. While Christians should never be harsh and unloving toward others, we should never compromise biblical truth just because the world considers God's sexual ethic narrow-minded and intolerant.

The truth is this: "The law of the LORD is perfect, reviving the soul; the testimony of the LORD is sure, making wise the simple" (Ps. 19:7).

DAY THREE

WORTH IT

I won't lie: following Jesus's ethic for love and sex isn't always easy. Many times it will clash with the culture around us. You've probably heard reports of Christian bakers, florists, and photographers who have been sued or put out of business for refusing to provide service for same-sex weddings. Maybe you'll never be in a position like theirs. But you may still be shamed and ostracized for choosing Jesus's sexual ethic over the culture's. This can be very discouraging, so we need to remind ourselves of God's promises for our lives. In the end, following Christ will be worth it.

READ ROMANS 8:28-29.

And we know that for those who love God all things work together for good, for those who are called according to his purpose. For those whom he foreknew he also predestined to be conformed to the image of his Son, in order that he might be the firstborn among many brothers.

What is the promise in these verses for those who love God?

What does it mean to be "conformed to the image of his Son"?

We get to become like Jesus. That is the goal of every Christian. But we don't accomplish this on our own—we have God's help along the way.

This passage doesn't begin by saying some things work together for good or just the minor things in our lives. No, *all* things work together for good. This means no matter what we go through—good or bad—every bit of it will work out for good in the end if we follow God and His purpose.

Paul didn't just write these words—he lived them. He had been beaten, shipwrecked, and imprisoned, and he faced constant dangers and difficulties throughout his life (see 2 Cor. 11). Yet he also said this:

READ 2 CORINTHIANS 4:16-18.

So we do not lose heart. Though our outer self is wasting away, our inner self is being renewed day by day. For this light momentary affliction is preparing for us an eternal weight of glory beyond all comparison, as we look not to the things that are seen but to the things that are unseen. For the things that are seen are transient, but the things that are unseen are eternal.

According to Paul, what is our motivation for not giving up?

What do these kinds of experiences do for us?

What must we keep in mind whenever we face difficult situations?

We can't always see what God is up to when we struggle. Still, we have to trust who we know Him to be. He is good, and all things work together for our good and His glory. He promises that you absolutely will face difficult circumstances, but He also promises that you will never face them alone. Our God is always with us, even in the trials.

He is a God we can trust—no matter what.

TRUE FREEDOM

START

Take some time to think about how you would answer this question: What does "freedom" mean?

Does freedom really mean the ability to do whatever we want?

It may seem like freedom is the ability to do whatever you would like, but is that really a good definition of freedom? Think about an instrument or a car. You can bang on the keys of a piano as loudly as you want, but is that real freedom? You are free to drive a car until it runs out of gas (or charge, if it's electric) but is that really freedom? As we prepare to watch the video teaching, let's see if this really is a good understanding of freedom.

WATCH

WATCH THE SESSION 2 VIDEO. FILL IN THE BLANKS AS YOU FOLLOW ALONG.

1. Freedom is not doing whatever we want, but freedom involves cultivating the _____ _____.

2. Freedom isn't acting without restraint but using something _____ to its _____.

3. If God exists, would that change anything about the _____ of _____?

4. Freedom is not doing whatever you want, but living according to _____ _____ for your life.

5. You and I are made for_____. We need a relationship with _____, and we need relationships with other _____.

6. We can only be _____ when we embrace the kinds of relationships—in the right manner—that God has _____ us for.

7. Freedom is _____ the right wants.

DISCUSS

According to the Christian worldview, true freedom is not a matter of doing whatever you want without restraint, but cultivating the right wants and living in obedience to God. In other words, freedom results when our wants align with God's.

Does that mean freedom comes through self-determination? No! If you try to be obedient through your own effort, you will fail. The Christian worldview uniquely teaches that we are incapable of living a God-honoring life in our own power. The reason is because sin has affected us to the core.

READ ROMANS 3:9-12,19-20.

What then? Are we Jews any better off? No, not at all. For we have already charged that all, both Jews and Greeks, are under sin, as it is written: "None is righteous, no, not one; no one understands; no one seeks for God. All have turned aside; together they have become worthless; no one does good, not even one." . . .

Now we know that whatever the law says it speaks to those who are under the law, so that every mouth may be stopped, and the whole world may be held accountable to God. For by works of the law no human being will be justified in his sight, since through the law comes knowledge of sin.

What harsh truth about the human condition is revealed in these verses?

Are we capable of reaching God through our own good works? Why or why not?

What does God's law show us?

In these verses, Paul reveals that all people have turned away from God and that no one, in and of themselves, is good. The purpose of the law then becomes to show us what is right and wrong. However, in no way does keeping the law gain us standing or righteousness before God.

The secret to the Christian life—and what separates Christianity from other religions—is found in grace. When we acknowledge our own brokenness and inability to live as God wants us to, He transforms our hearts and lives. Our strength comes in acknowledging our weakness and failure and depending on God. GOOD NEWS!

Now let's revisit our original question about what it means to be free. Since God is personal, and He exists, does that change how we understand freedom?

Do you think believing in God makes a person feel more or less free? Why?

Maybe you think believing in God adds guilt in this life or judgment when you die. Maybe you think God's existence makes no significant difference in someone feeling free—except for the weight of the consequences that result from poor choices.

But the existence of a personal God changes everything.

The world is not a cosmic accident but is purposefully fashioned by a Creator. In fact, the first thing we learn about God in the Bible is that He is the Creator (see Gen. 1:1). Just like a car that has been designed to operate a certain way—and is only "free" when used correctly—humans have also been created for a greater purpose and only experience real freedom when they discover and live that purpose.

What do you think God has made us for? What is our purpose?

READ GENESIS 1:26-27.

Then God said, "Let us make man in our image, after our likeness. And let them have dominion over the fish of the sea and over the birds of the heavens and over the livestock and over all the earth and over every creeping thing that creeps on the earth." So God created man in his own image, in the image of God he created him; male and female he created them.

Highlight or circle the phrases "our image" and "our likeness." What does being made in God's image have to do with our purpose?

Scripture often mentions God being known by the people He created. Read the following verses and see.

READ THE FOLLOWING SCRIPTURES.

"And I will walk among you and will be your God, and you shall be my people." — *Leviticus 26:12*

"But let him who boasts boast in this, that he understands and knows me, that I am the LORD who practices steadfast love, justice, and righteousness in the earth. For in these things I delight, declares the LORD." — *Jeremiah 9:24*

"I will give them a heart to know that I am the LORD, and they shall be my people and I will be their God, for they shall return to me with their whole heart." — Jeremiah 24:7

See what kind of love the Father has given to us, that we should be called children of God; and so we are. —1 John 3:1

In this is love, not that we have loved God but that he loved us and sent his Son to be the propitiation for our sins. —1 John 4:10

After reading all of these verses, what do they reveal about God's relationship with us?

In what ways does God's relationship with us model how we should relate to others?

Scripture reveals that God made us for relationship with Him and with others. As we learned in the last session, Jesus said the greatest commandments are to love God and love others (see Mark 12). True freedom exists in healthy, intimate relationships with both God and other people. Therefore, the free and abundant life Jesus offers us can only be experienced through these committed relationships, rooted and grown in God's intended design.

Throughout the creation story in Genesis, God consistently called His creation "good." Yet there is one thing God said is not good.

Then the LORD God said, "It is not good that the man should be alone; I will make him a helper fit for him."

Why do you think it is not good for a person to be alone, apart from human relationships and connection?

We know God created us to be in relationship with Him, and we know Adam needed Eve to multiply and fill the earth (see Gen. 1:28). But God also made humans to be in relationship with other human beings. We are not meant to live in isolation. We are designed to live in families and communities with other people.

Since we are made for relationships, we can only be truly free through commitment and faithfulness. This may seem counterintuitive. After all, we live in a world of endless options. From consumer products, to music, to streaming TV, you can seemingly have whatever you want, when you want it, how you want it, and with whomever you want. The world often asks: *Why not give up on difficult relationships? In terms of marriage, why commit to one person for life? Why limit yourself?*

What problems arise from a lack of faithfulness and commitment?

How are faithfulness and commitments actually freeing?

Is there someone that you know will always stick by your side, no matter what? If so, what would your life be like without him or her?

There is comfort in knowing someone always has your back, whether it is a spouse when you are older or a close friend right now. True faithfulness and commitment assure us that someone won't leave us at the first sign of trouble and that we will work through problems together.

Let's revisit our original question: What does it mean to be truly free?

Instead of being restrictive, how do committed relationships actually bring us greater freedom?

God invites each one of us to the freedom that comes from committing our lives to His purpose for us and loving other people in relationship. This is the only path to experiencing the truly rich life Jesus invited us to live.

DAY ONE
PRACTICE

Many people who have abandoned their faith did so because they thought it was too restrictive—often in matters of sexuality. But as we've learned, abandoning God does not grant us freedom; true freedom only comes through following God's will for our lives.

We also know that following God's plan isn't always easy. Paul knew this well, which is why he said, "For when I am weak, then I am strong" (2 Cor. 12:10). At first glance, this may seem like a contradiction. But let's look at the verse in context.

READ 2 CORINTHIANS 12:9-10.

But [the Lord] said to me, "My grace is sufficient for you, for my power is made perfect in weakness." Therefore I will boast all the more gladly of my weaknesses, so that the power of Christ may rest upon me. For the sake of Christ, then, I am content with weaknesses, insults, hardships, persecutions, and calamities. For when I am weak, then I am strong.

Where does our power to do what is right come from?

What does this passage teach you about your own weaknesses and shortcomings?

Paul knew the power of the Christian life comes when we rely on the power of Christ to work through us. God's grace and power carry us forward.

But letting go of our need to accomplish things our own way isn't easy—this is why spiritual disciplines are so important. Maybe the term "spiritual disciplines" is unfamiliar to you. These are actions or daily practices that help us grow our relationship with God. Just as freedom comes to a piano player who practices on a regular basis, freedom comes to the Christian who "practices" the spiritual life.

What are the ways some Christians "practice" the spiritual life?

If you get stuck, here are some spiritual disciplines mentioned in Scripture.

- Prayer (Matt. 6:5-6)
- Fasting (Matt. 6:16-18)
- Solitude (Ps. 46:10; Mark 1:35)
- Service (Gal. 5:13-14; 1 Pet. 4:10)
- Stewardship (Matt. 25:23,29)
- Bible Study (2 Tim. 3:16)
- Fellowship (Acts 2:42)

- Confession (James 5:16; 1 John 1:9)
- Worship (1 Chron. 16:29; Rom. 12:1-2)
- Rest (Matt. 11:28-30)
- Generosity (Acts 20:35)
- Purity (Phil. 4:8; 1 Thess. 4:3-4)
- Evangelism (Matt. 28:19-20)

TAKE A MINUTE TO LOOK UP THE SCRIPTURE REFERENCES LISTED WITH EACH DISCIPLINE TO HELP YOU UNDERSTAND IT BETTER.

Which of these disciplines do you "practice" most?

Which of these disciplines are missing in your life? Ask God to help you develop them.

Spiritual disciplines are vital for cultivating the kind of character in which our wants align with God's. But remember that God is the One who ultimately brings transformation in our hearts through grace.

READ PHILIPPIANS 2:12-13.

Therefore, my beloved, as you have always obeyed, so now, not only as in my presence but much more in my absence, work out your own salvation with fear and trembling, for it is God who works in you, both to will and to work for his good pleasure.

These verses don't mean we have to work for our salvation. They mean we grow in our relationship with God by respecting Him, by doing things in our lives that help us know Him more (such as spiritual disciplines), and by engaging in things that please Him.

How will you "work out" your salvation today?

DAY TWO
NO STRINGS ATTACHED?

What are some ways you've heard the Christian view on sex described in our culture? *Relationships*

Be honest: Do you agree with any of these things?

You've probably listed things such as "old fashioned," "repressive," or even "unhealthy." Maybe you even agree with some of these views. But have you ever stopped to think about all of the harmful results—both for the individual and society—that come from rejecting Jesus's sexual ethic?

One of the messages our society shares about sex is that sex outside of marriage is okay as long as it's consensual. But "casual" sex has negative consequences—physical and emotional.

What are some of the negative physical consequences to casual sex?

Some obvious responses are sexually transmitted infections (STIs) and unwanted pregnancies. But what are the long-term consequences? An STI can impact your health for the rest of your life. When faced with an unwanted pregnancy, a woman must choose whether to keep the child, adopt, or abort. These are all extremely difficult situations, with the last one causing the death of an innocent unborn child.

Now, how many of us think about the *emotional* consequences of sex? Even if it is consensual and intended to be "no strings attached," is that ever really the case?

What are the negative emotional consequences of casual sex?

Even when sex is consensual, it can lead to guilt or shame. A person may feel used or even violated. Maybe a sexual encounter that was supposed to be "no strings attached" generated an emotional connection to a person who doesn't feel the same in return, leading to feelings of rejection. This means there are also relational consequences to casual sex.

What are other negative relational consequences of casual sex?

Casual sex can make a friendship or work environment awkward, cause emotional distress, and be seriously damaging, especially if one of the people involved is in a committed relationship or even has a family. An affair has tons of negative consequences, from emotional pain to loss of trust to feelings of inadequacy. It can tear a family apart, affecting both adults and children emotionally, psychologically, and spiritually.

Until now, we have only examined the effects of consensual sex. Unfortunately, not all sexual activity is consensual. Abusive sexual activity is a terrible thing, but it occurs all too often. As awful as these things are, we need to talk about them.

What are the results of a person ignoring another's consent in sexual activity?

You've probably listed things such as sexual harassment and rape. Maybe you think of the #MeToo movement. Or maybe you've even listed sexual slavery and human trafficking. These are all terrible things that happen when people reject the intrinsic value of human beings and simply use people for their own pleasure.

Many people view the Christian sexual ethic as old-fashioned or repressive. But look at all of the harmful consequences that can—and do—occur by ignoring it. God never intended for any of these things to happen.

Now let's end on a positive note. We've examined the harm that comes from ignoring Jesus's sexual ethic. Let's look at the good that results from following it.

What are positive consequences of following Jesus's sexual ethic? Don't just think about the lack of the things listed above. Think of the positive individual and societal outcomes that result from healthy sexual activity as God intended.

Following the Christian sexual ethic means strong, healthy families and societies; commitment, trust, security; and freedom and abundant life. There are more positive results than we can imagine, but know this: God's design is for our good.

DAY THREE
FREE TO LIVE

Freedom is a major theme in this week's study. We've explored how true freedom comes from following God's rules instead of rejecting them. Today, we'll talk about the importance of perspective when it comes to freedom. Look back at Genesis 2.

READ GENESIS 2:15-17.

The LORD God took the man and put him in the garden of Eden to work it and keep it. And the LORD God commanded the man, saying, "You may surely eat of every tree of the garden, but of the tree of the knowledge of good and evil you shall not eat, for in the day that you eat of it you shall surely die."

What was Adam free to do?

What was the one thing he was not permitted to do?

Which was greater: Adam's freedom or his restriction? Why?

Adam was free to eat from any tree in the entire garden—except one. Only one. But humanity fell when Satan tempted Adam and Eve to disobey God's one restriction.

READ GENESIS 3:1.

Now the serpent was more crafty than any other beast of the field that the LORD God had made. He said to the woman, "Did God actually say, 'You shall not eat of any tree in the garden'?"

Compare this to what God said in Genesis 2:15-17.

How did God and the serpent begin each of their statements?

God: "You may _____ eat of _____ tree of the _____."

Serpent: "Did God _____ say, 'You shall _____ eat of _____ tree in the garden'?"

What did God focus on first? What did the serpent focus on? Think specifically about the way their statements relate to freedom and restrictions.

How did the serpent's description of God's one restriction compare to what God actually said?

What does this say about how we tend to view God's rules?

Satan wants us to focus on everything we aren't allowed to do rather than everything we are free to do. He wants to magnify God's restrictions so we'll think God is oppressive. Satan wants us to think God is withholding something good from us instead of protecting us from things that are bad.

Does this sound familiar? Our society is still falling for Satan's deception. We think God's rules are harsh and limiting. But disobeying God's sexual ethic causes so much harm to us and society as a whole. God's design for sex does not restrict us; it protects us.

Are you ready to trust that God knows best?

REAL
LOVE

START

What is love? Endless songs, movies, and poems are about "true love." But can you define it? If not, how could you really know if you love someone? How could you know if you can really believe someone who says, "I love you"?

Write out your own definition of love.

Do you typically view love more in terms of emotions or behaviors? Explain.

In this session, we will explore what love truly means and how we can love people with both our bodies and our souls.

WATCH

WATCH THE SESSION 3 VIDEO. FILL IN THE BLANKS AS YOU FOLLOW ALONG.

1. _____ means to provide the best for someone, to develop to _____ —physically, emotionally, relationally, spiritually.

2. Cherish means to _____ something.

3. _____ is to protect and provide.

4. Love involves being committed to the _____ of another person, regardless of how they _____.

5. _____ knows what is best for us.

6. We are called to be kind, gracious, and loving toward other _____. But we also have to act with a confidence that God's design is _____.

7. It's truth that brings freedom, but we're to present that _____ in _____.

8. What we do with our bodies and how we treat people _____.

DISCUSS

My father shared a definition of love with me when I was a teen that has helped me throughout my life. If you take the time to understand it and commit it to heart, it can be a game-changer for your life and relationships:

READ EPHESIANS 5:25-29.

> *Husbands, love your wives, as Christ loved the church and gave himself up for her, that he might sanctify her, having cleansed her by the washing of water with the word, so that he might present the church to himself in splendor, without spot or wrinkle or any such thing, that she might be holy and without blemish. In the same way husbands should love their wives as their own bodies. He who loves his wife loves himself. For no one ever hated his own flesh, but nourishes and cherishes it, just as Christ does the church.*

While this teaches specifically about the love of a husband for his wife, it still teaches us a lot about love in general.

In these verses, who is the ultimate example of how to love?

How did Christ love the church?

What does it mean to nourish and cherish our bodies?

How can we nourish and cherish those we love?

Put these two words together—*nourish* and *cherish*—and we have the simple definition of love my father shared with me: to protect and provide. Biblical love, which is rooted in Jesus's sacrificial love, aims to protect loved ones from harm and to provide for their good.

We saw in the last session how living out Jesus's sexual ethic would transform societies for the better, but it is also good for individuals. God gives us commands about sex to protect and provide for us, not to steal our fun.

Consider how following God's loving commands to reserve sex for the unity of a man and woman in marriage both protect and provide for us.

What does reserving sex for marriage protect us from?

What does it provide for us?

God wants to protect us from physical, emotional, and spiritual harm and to provide us with genuine freedom in our relationships. Marriage is intended to do just that—give us the freedom to express our love as God designed it, a beautiful unity between one man and one woman for life.

How does loving others God's way actually give us freedom?

Our hearts don't always align with God's standards, though. Given the power of sin, it is easy for us to be confused about what is right and what is wrong in our dating relationships and even in marriage.

How do we love people who may not even realize what they are doing is wrong?

What does it look like to love people who reject the biblical understanding of love and embrace another version? How do we love people who think Christians are judgmental and intolerant?

Remember, true love is not a feeling, but a commitment to do what's best for others, even if they don't recognize or accept the reality of what's best for them. In other words, loving others doesn't necessarily imply that they will recognize we are protecting and providing for them.

Many people may even confuse loving actions for hateful ones. After all, people made fun of Jesus on the cross. Love involves being committed to the good of others regardless of how they feel.

Share about a time when you spoke the truth in love and someone else saw it as hateful or judgmental. What happened? How was the truth you shared for that person's good?

Now, think of a time when someone confronted you in love about a difficult truth. How did you respond? How would you respond differently now, knowing it was an act of love?

God knows what is best for all of us—and He is the designer and creator of sex. He knows what's best for you, what's best for me, and what's best for our neighbors. Does this mean we get to be the morality police, criticizing others who don't follow the biblical sexual ethic? No, that's not the point. We begin by loving them, and if loving them means seeking their best, our words will not always be received well. What the world says is best rarely aligns with God's best for us. But knowing what real love is gives us courage to speak truth, even when it's unpopular.

READ WHAT JESUS SAID IN JOHN 8:32 ABOUT THE TRUTH.
"You will know the truth, and the truth will set you free."

How exactly does the truth set us free? What does it set us free from, and what does it set us free to do?

We don't speak truth to sound smart, win an argument, or silence people. We speak truth because truth brings freedom. When we speak truth, we are called to speak it in love, as Jesus did.

Yes, God calls us to tell the truth and to say it with love. Still, we can go too far on both sides of this equation. We mess up by speaking truth without grace-filled kindness and genuine concern for others. And we can also make the mistake of watering down truth so we don't offend anyone.

In what cultural issues do you think it is especially important to properly balance truth and grace?

Jesus invites us to this balancing act of grace and truth in all areas of our lives. To balance well, we need to learn how to love people with both our bodies and our souls.

One of the lies our culture tells is that we can separate the physical part of being human (the body) from the spiritual part (the soul). The world says the body carries no meaning on its own, and we can do with it whatever we want or think. But life doesn't work that way. We all know that the actions we carry out with our bodies have meaning. We can tell the truth with our words yet still lie with our bodies.

> **Think of the ways we use our bodies to interact with people (for example, a handshake or a pat on the back) and the messages we convey by those actions. What else can you think of? What do those actions communicate?**

If what we do with our bodies communicates something, then what about sex? Does this action communicate something deeper or is sex really "just for fun" as many seem to believe?

> **Let's talk about this question for a minute. Think back to this session's video and all you've learned so far. Now, think about it: Is sex really "just for fun"?**

We communicate with our bodies and our words because God has made us both body and soul. God formed Adam from "the dust in the ground," breathed into him "the breath of life," and then he became a "living being" (Gen. 2:7). So, a human being has both a physical dimension (body) and a spiritual dimension (soul). We are bodily beings animated by a soul.

> **What positive changes can you expect in your own relationships when you begin to show love for others with both your body and soul?**

Here's the bottom line: Sex means something. Physical touch means something. Our bodies and souls both matter. We must ask ourselves this: How do we honor God and love other people with our bodies and our souls?

DAY ONE

DRESSED FOR HONOR

When it comes to sex, two words are commonly used in student ministry: modesty and purity. Those conversations tend to be awkward for both leaders and students. But it's important to be clear on these ideas because we often misunderstand what they mean.

Write out definitions for the following in your own words:

- **Modesty:**

- **Purity:**

When we discuss modesty, we typically talk about the way people dress. While you might want to roll your eyes when you hear the word *modesty*, it is actually important for a healthy sexual ethic. Think about it this way: If we are called to honor God with our bodies, then shouldn't this influence how we dress? Out of respect for our brothers and sisters in Christ, who aim to love God in both thought and deed, shouldn't we dress with modesty? Although this teaching is often directed at girls, guys need it too.

We are all responsible for our own lustful thoughts. But does this mean we have no responsibility to one another about how we present our bodies? Do we have God-honoring motives when we dress in a way that invites others to look at us with lust? Modesty asks us to consider that how we dress contributes to the broader environment. So we ask ourselves: How can we dress in a way that brings honor to God and helps create a loving environment for others?

Take a minute to think about your own life and how you dress. Are you dressing in a way that brings honor to God and shows love to others? Explain.

For some, the word "purity" carries baggage. The idea of living in a pure way becomes misguided when it is a means to shame people rather than a way to encourage others to live within the abundance of God's grace. That doesn't mean we can throw purity out the window. In fact, let's see what the Bible has to say about purity and sexual immorality.

READ 1 CORINTHIANS 6:19-20.

Or do you not know that your body is a temple of the Holy Spirit within you, whom you have from God? You are not your own, for you were bought with a price. So glorify God in your body.

What does Paul say your body is? Why is this important to sexual purity?

Our culture likes to say, "I can do whatever I want with my body." What do these verses reveal about this mentality?

What do these verses say we must do with our bodies?

God's commands are for our good, and we thrive when we live as God has designed us to live. The motivation to avoid sexual immorality isn't about us. Rather, the motivation should be to honor God with our bodies. The question should be, "How do we best use our bodies to love God and love other people?"

Ask yourself: *Am I honoring God with my body*? **Write a few sentences in response.**

DAY TWO

BALANCE

Finding the balance between grace and truth is not always easy. Your generation faces difficult ethical questions that previous generations never had to consider.

DESCRIBE HOW YOU WOULD RESPOND IN THE FOLLOWING SITUATIONS WITH TRUTH AND GRACE.

You are invited to a same-sex wedding. Do you attend out of love for your friend or family member or do you decline because it goes against God's model for marriage?

A transgender classmate wishes to be addressed by her or his preferred gender pronoun. Do you comply out of grace or does that reject the biological truth?

Scripture does not give us simple answers, but Jesus invites us to follow His lead by responding with both grace and truth. He invites us to truly love people, whether they realize we're loving them or not. Let's see how He exemplified this.

READ MARK 2:15-17.

And as he reclined at table in his house, many tax collectors and sinners were reclining with Jesus and his disciples, for there were many who followed him. And the scribes of the Pharisees, when they saw that he was eating with sinners and tax collectors, said to his disciples, "Why does he eat with tax collectors and sinners?" And when Jesus heard it, he said to them, "Those who are well have no need of a physician, but those who are sick. I came not to call the righteous, but sinners."

Why did the Pharisees criticize Jesus? How did Jesus explain eating with "sinners"?

Why was it important that Jesus ate with known "sinners"? What would this accomplish?

Jesus was criticized for dining with "tax collectors and sinners." Since they were "sinners," Jesus knew they would be more open to His message than self-righteous religious leaders. Rather than requiring them to change their moral behavior first, He built loving relationships with them, knowing they could only experience spiritual transformation *after* they experienced His grace.

Here's another example of Jesus exercising grace and truth.

READ JOHN 4:7-18 IN YOUR BIBLE.

Why did the woman find it odd that Jesus was speaking with her?

How did Jesus exercise both grace and truth with the Samaritan woman?

In both scenarios, Jesus interacted with people who the social and religious traditions of His day said He shouldn't associate with. This shows Jesus's great love for everyone, including those society shunned. Because He showed them grace, He was then able to share truth.

What do these two interactions of Jesus with "sinners" teach us about how we can love others with grace and truth?

Think of someone in your life who isn't living according to God's sexual ethic. List some practical ways you can show this person grace and truth.

Once people know we love them, they may also be more open for us to share the truth with them. By loving them well, we show that we truly want what is best for them, just like God does.

DAY THREE
YOUR BODY MATTERS

One of the first heresies in the early church, Gnosticism, viewed the body as evil. Gnostics believed that salvation occurs when the soul escapes the "prison house" of the body.[1] But this is incredibly unbiblical. Genesis 1 tells us that creation—including the human body—is good.

With that in mind, consider the importance of Jesus taking on a human form.

READ THE FOLLOWING SCRIPTURES.

For we do not have a high priest who is unable to sympathize with our weaknesses, but one who in every respect has been tempted as we are, yet without sin. — Hebrews 4:15

"For God so loved the world, that he gave his only Son, that whoever believes in him should not perish but have eternal life." — John 3:16

"Greater love has no one than this, that someone lay down his life for his friends." — John 15:13

What was Jesus able to show us and do for us by taking on a human body?

Jesus took on human flesh to identity with us, to show us how to love, and ultimately to redeem us. This is why Scripture calls us to love God and others with our bodies and our souls. One way we love God with our souls is by learning to think like Christ.

READ ROMANS 12:2.

Do not be conformed to this world, but be transformed by the renewal of your mind, that by testing you may discern what is the will of God, what is good and acceptable and perfect.

What does the "renewal of your mind" mean? What does this enable us to avoid?

What does a renewed mind empower us to do?

We are transformed in part by learning to see the world through a biblical perspective. This is one of the main goals of this book—to help you think with the mind of Christ about sex, love, and relationships.

But we can't stop there. Not only are we called to renew our minds and transform our thinking, but we are also called to responsibly steward—that is, manage or care for—our bodies.

READ ROMANS 6:13 (CSB).

And do not offer any parts of [your body] to sin as weapons for unrighteousness. But as those who are alive from the dead, offer yourselves to God, and all the parts of yourselves to God as weapons for righteousness.

How does this relate to properly taking care of your body?

In other words, as believers, we have died to sin and been born as new creations in Christ. Our "old selves" were crucified with Christ and we have been set free by grace to honor God with our bodies (see Rom. 6:6).

List some actions and behaviors you resolve to do—or stop doing—so that you can honor God with your body.

GOD'S GRACE

START

Let's face it, the church has a bad reputation in our culture when it comes to sex and our view of those who have different beliefs.

What are the key differences between a biblical view of sex and how many in the world see it?

Why do you think the church has a bad reputation when it comes to sex? Is it simply because of what the Bible teaches? Explain.

In this session we will explore God's grace and how it can change your life.

WATCH

WATCH THE SESSION 4 VIDEO. FILL IN THE BLANKS AS YOU FOLLOW ALONG.

1. The Bible says the _Gospel_ is offensive.

2. When we _fail_ to live out the gospel, it undermines our credibility in a world that desperately _need_ the gospel.

3. Sometimes as Christians, we are quick to _judge_; we are quick to treat people in an un-Christlike manner because maybe we don't really _understand_ how much God has forgiven us.

4. Oftentimes we're uncharitable toward the world around us because we haven't first experienced _God's_ _grace_ in our life.

5. No matter your _past_, Jesus died for you. Jesus forgives you.

DISCUSS

Satan is intent on twisting God's good design for sex. Sex brings new life into the world, but Satan is a murderer and a liar (see John 8:44). Children are a blessing that bring hope for the future, but Satan wants people to be filled with hopelessness. Satan is opposed to God at every turn and has focused his work on undermining the goodness, truth, and beauty of sex.

To understand Satan's schemes, we need to go back to the creation story in Genesis and see what it reveals about his character. Genesis 1 repeatedly says creation is good. However, in Genesis 3, Satan shows up and tries to wreck God's plans for the world. He deceives Adam and Eve and tempts them into disobedience. As a result, sin enters the world and brings immeasurable suffering and calamity with it.

Take a look at Satan's strategy: he corrupts, deceives, and twists. Satan takes what God has made good and corrupts it. As the father of lies, Satan corrupts goodness and truth.

LIST SOME WAYS SATAN CORRUPTS THE FOLLOWING:

Biblical marriage:

Natural human sexual desires:

God's design for humans as gendered beings:

Satan corrupts biblical marriage by encouraging divorce. He corrupts natural human desires through pornography. He corrupts God's design for humans as gendered beings by threatening the objective reality of male and female. Satan is a corrupter of good.

But how does Satan corrupt these good things? He infects what God has made good with his lies. Put simply: he deceives us.

READ GENESIS 3:1-4.

Now the serpent was more crafty than any other beast of the field that the LORD God had made. He said to the woman, "Did God actually say, 'You shall not eat of any tree in the garden'?" And the woman said to the serpent, "We may eat of the fruit of the trees in the garden, but God said, 'You shall not eat of the fruit of the tree that is in the midst of the garden, neither shall you touch it, lest you die.'" But the serpent said to the woman, "You will not surely die."

In what ways did Satan undermine God in these verses?

Satan asked Adam and Eve questions to subtly break down their confidence in God's character. Satan appeared as a snake in the garden, but since this was before the fall into sin, they didn't suspect anything unusual.

READ 2 CORINTHIANS 11:14.

And no wonder, for even Satan disguises himself as an angel of light.

Satan doesn't wear a red suit and carry a pitchfork. I don't think many people truly believe he is this cartoon-like character. But I am concerned that they are being unknowingly influenced with unbiblical ideas through music, movies, social media, friends, and a host of other mediums. Why? Because Satan's deception isn't obvious. He didn't tell Adam and Eve not to trust what God said; instead, he asked questions that made them doubt.

Not only does Satan disguise his deception, but he is also clever about the way he presents it. Think about Adam and Eve: he talked them into doing the wrong thing and convinced them what they were doing was right. He does the same thing today: he can convince people to make wrong choices and believe that their wrong choices are actually the right ones.

Satan twists God's words until we're confused about what God actually said to us. This is why we must not measure God's Word by our feelings, but rather measure our feelings by God's Word.

What was the first question Satan asked Eve in Genesis 3:1-4?

What did God actually command in Genesis 2:16-17?

The first question Satan asked Adam and Eve was about the words God had spoken. Sadly, Adam and Eve bought into his twisted interpretation of God's Word and ate the fruit. But when Jesus was tempted, He quoted Scripture—God's Word—back to Satan (see Matt: 4:3-10; Luke 4:3-12). Jesus knew Satan would twist God's words and that freedom only comes from aligning our lives with the truth of Scripture.

Satan still operates with this same strategy of corrupting God's good design, deceiving people about His character and twisting His Word. And God's sexual ethic is one of Satan's targets.

Before we explore God's specific design for sex, singleness, and marriage, it is important to take a minute to make sure we clearly understand God's love and forgiveness and have that clear in our own hearts.

How does personally experiencing and understanding God's grace influence the way we treat others?

How does it influence the way we view ourselves?

Without personally experiencing God's grace and forgiveness, we become incapable of genuinely loving others. When we understand how much grace God has shown us, we can more easily extend grace to others.

Earlier we talked about what culture thinks about the church's sexual ethics. Christians are often accused of being harsh, judgmental, homophobic, hateful, and narrow-minded toward those who hold a different sexual ethic. Sometimes these claims are dishonest strategies meant to silence and shame Christians for their views.

But sometimes these claims are true. The church has often failed to live as God desires us to live. Porn is an issue in the church. Some people have been treated poorly because they struggle with same-sex attraction. There has been gossip, pride, lust, divorce, and so on. The church is not immune to the sins of the world. And, by the way, the church is not a building— it's made up of all of God's people, including you and me.

It's also easy to get trapped in a cycle of guilt and shame rather than experiencing the freedom that comes in Christ through God's grace and forgiveness.

Imagine that a friend—even someone sitting next to you right now—is struggling with guilt and shame. What would you say to that friend?

I have had countless conversations with young people who are overwhelmed by guilt and shame. So many of them feel like "used goods" or a "hopeless cause" because of their past sexual activity, an addiction to porn, or some other struggle in their lives. My response is always the same:

> *God loves you. Yes, He calls you to repent and turn from your sins, exchanging your way for His design. But when you confess your sins—fully turning your life over to Him, rather than just saying you're sorry—God is faithful and just to forgive you. Jesus wants you to be free from shame and guilt, which is why He invited those who are weighed down and exhausted to come to Him for rest. That includes you.*

We can be confident in God's love and forgiveness because of what Jesus did on the cross. Crucifixion was the most painful and shameful death imaginable. Even though He was innocent, Jesus was willingly crucified for you and me.

OPEN YOUR BIBLE AND READ HEBREWS 2:18; 4:15.

What was the purpose of Jesus's testing and suffering?

When you feel weak or when you are being tested, what should you tell yourself?

No matter what you have done or what has been done to you, if you trust Jesus for forgiveness, please know that God forgives you. God is not a harsh King who enjoys judging us, but a loving heavenly Father who wants us to be in relationship with Him and other people—and to experience the freedom that comes from forgiveness. God wants you to have a fresh start. And that fresh start can begin today.

DAY ONE
SOUL CREATION

I recently asked a group of students these questions. How would you respond to them?

What kinds of human creations last the longest?

Can humans create anything that lasts forever?

Students answered the first question with things such as archaeological remains: the Egyptian pyramids, Machu Pichu, and so forth. But they all agreed that the answer to the second question is no. After all, everything eventually falls apart. Even though I pressed them for an answer, they concluded that humans are incapable of creating anything that lasts forever.

But I told them: "I think you are missing something. With God's power, humans can make something that lasts forever—another human being."

As we've talked about, I also explained to them that God made humans as both body and soul (see Matt. 10:28). Physical things in this world do fade away, including our bodies, but each person has an eternal soul that will never cease to exist. A trillion years from now, you will have just as much time left in eternity as you do today. That sounds crazy, right?

This is why "sex is the most powerful creative act in the universe. When a man and a woman come together in a sexual relationship, the possibility of creating an eternal soul/spirit arises. At the moment of conception, a new immortal soul/spirit has entered into eternity."[1] Take a minute to let this point sink in. Seriously, re-read those last few sentences and make sure you don't miss this: God has created human beings with the capacity to create something that lasts forever—another human being.

How does this change the way you view sex?

As C. S. Lewis said, there are no ordinary people. "You have never talked to a mere mortal. Nations, cultures, arts, civilization—these are mortal, and their life is to ours as the life of a gnat. But it is immortals whom we joke with, work with, marry, snub, and exploit—immortal horrors or everlasting splendors." [2]

With sex, two people engage in an activity that has the potential to create another "immortal" being. The eternal nature of human beings is one reason sex is so sacred and powerful.

What does this teach you about yourself and the things you value in life?

How should we view and treat other people as a result of what we have learned today?

DAY TWO
NOT THE WORST

Sex is a big deal. But Satan twists this reality through a variety of cultural mediums, presenting sex as the biggest deal.

Think about the songs, movies, commercials, memes, and GIFs that you encounter on a regular basis. What are the various messages these things offer about sex?

What is your view of sex? How important is it to your personal happiness?

The sexual revolution has tried to convince us that sex is *the* route to happiness. Sex is undoubtedly good and a wonderful gift from God, but it is not the be-all and end-all of human existence.

Satan has also convinced some believers that sex outside marriage is the worst sin—that it is practically unforgivable. Sadly, many Christians have adopted a twisted view of God's Word that makes sexual sinners out to be incapable of experiencing God's best. But this is also a lie. You need to know that you are loved and forgiven—no matter your sin.

Have you ever felt so guilty or judged by others that you thought you were incapable of experiencing God's best? Explain.

Have you ever had a hard time believing you are forgiven? Why?

READ 1 CORINTHIANS 6:9-11 IN YOUR BIBLE.

What sins had some of the people in Corinth committed in the past?

What is their status in God's eyes now? What does this say for anyone who has fallen short of Jesus's sexual ethic?

Before they were Christians, some Corinthian believers engaged in a range of sexually immoral behavior—such as adultery and homosexual behavior—but Paul still describes them as "washed," "sanctified," and "justified in the name of the Lord Jesus Christ" (1 Cor. 6:11). Sexual sin is serious, and it brings consequences—but it is not the worst sin, and it is certainly not unforgivable. If participating in this study so far has brought up some pain from your own sexual failures, please know God forgives you when you ask.

READ 1 JOHN 1:9.

If we confess our sins, he is faithful and just to forgive us our sins and to cleanse us from all unrighteousness.

What two words are used to describe God in these verses?

What two things does God promise if we confess our sins?

READ 1 TIMOTHY 1:15-16.

The saying is trustworthy and deserving of full acceptance, that Christ Jesus came into the world to save sinners, of whom I am the foremost. But I received mercy for this reason, that in me, as the foremost, Jesus Christ might display his perfect patience as an example to those who were to believe in him for eternal life.

Why did Jesus come into the world?

What does this passage say about God and His feelings toward us?

Even the apostle Paul, who considered himself "the worst of sinners," said God came into the world through Jesus to save sinners (see 1 Tim. 1:15). This includes you and me.

If you are willing to confess, ask God to forgive you, and turn away from your sins, then you can begin to experience true freedom in Christ. The Christian story is about a loving heavenly Father who relentlessly pursues us because He wants to see each of us transformed through the power of His grace.

DAY THREE

NO SHAME

Yesterday, we discussed how Jesus's sacrifice makes forgiveness for our sexual sins possible. We also learned how Jesus relates to us in our trials and suffering because He was tested and suffered (see Heb. 2:18; 4:15). But how can He really understand the shame that comes from sexual sins?

Jesus suffered great physical pain during His crucifixion. But did you know victims of crucifixion were also stripped naked to further humiliate them? With this in mind, let's go back to Genesis 3—to the moments right after Adam and Eve ate from the tree God commanded them not to.

READ GENESIS 3:7-8.

Then the eyes of both were opened, and they knew that they were naked. And they sewed fig leaves together and made themselves loincloths. And they heard the sound of the LORD God walking in the garden in the cool of the day, and the man and his wife hid themselves from the presence of the LORD God among the trees of the garden.

What was Adam and Eve's first realization after they sinned?

How did they respond to their realization?

What did Adam and Eve do when they heard God walking in the garden? Why do you think they did this?

When Adam and Eve sinned in the garden, they hid and covered themselves with fig leaves to hide their shame. Look at what God did in response.

READ GENESIS 3:21.

And the LORD God made for Adam and for his wife garments of skins and clothed them.

From what did God make Adam and Eve's new clothing?

What would God need to do to make this possible?

Why do you think God did this? What would it have taught Adam and Eve?

God exchanged Adam and Eve's fig leaves with the covering of animal skin, which was the first death in Scripture. But then in the ultimate act of redemption, God covered their nakedness through His own nakedness on the cross. Jesus willingly experienced the depth of human sin through public torture, humiliation, and nakedness so we could experience freedom from shame. Jesus held nothing back so we could be forgiven.

What does this teach you about any shame you may experience?

What should you do in response to guilt and shame?

GOD'S DESIGN

START

Jesus was a sexual being.

Do you think this is true? What is your immediate reaction to this statement?

Does this claim strike you as bizarre? Maybe even heretical? Let me explain. Christians often fail to reflect on how Jesus's humanity should inform our understanding of sexuality. We focus on Jesus as divine and tend to forget He was also completely human just like us—except for one way: He was completely sinless.

WATCH

WATCH THE SESSION 5 VIDEO. FILL IN THE BLANKS AS YOU FOLLOW ALONG.

1. When we know why God made _____, and we take that to heart, then we're _____.

2. Part of the purpose of sex is to procreate, multiply, and fill the _____.

3. Sex is about bonding two people together—a _____ and his _____ —in a permanent relationship.

4. The one-flesh union is a beautiful image of our _____ union with God.

5. The craving of the human heart _____ be fulfilled by sex.

6. The deepest cry in the human heart is for _____ —to know and to be known.

7. Myth 1: Sex is not a _____ _____.

8. Myth 2: Sex is just a _____ act.

9. _____ is the context in which God has given us sex.

DISCUSS

Have you ever questioned whether Jesus—God in the flesh—was really human? Why or why not?

Jesus didn't pretend to be human; He didn't just put on a human body and disguise Himself as a man. He became a man to walk on earth among people.

READ HEBREWS 2:14,17-18 (CSB).

Now since the children have flesh and blood in common, Jesus also shared in these, so that through his death he might destroy the one holding the power of death—that is, the devil. . . . Therefore, he had to be like his brothers and sisters in every way, so that he could become a merciful and faithful high priest in matters pertaining to God, to make atonement for the sins of the people. For since he himself has suffered when he was tempted, he is able to help those who are tempted.

According to these verses, why did Jesus become human?

Scripture teaches that Jesus was human in every way—eating, sleeping, being tempted—yet He was without sin. Jesus was both fully God and fully human.

This means Jesus, like the rest of us, was a sexual being. This doesn't mean He was sexually active, but it does mean that Jesus had sexual characteristics. When God chose to fully reveal Himself to us, He entered into the human race with a fully human body, affirming the goodness of human sexuality.

But Jesus didn't stop at coming into the world as a man. He also came into human nature through the womb of a woman.

Why do you think it's important that Jesus was born from a woman?

Jesus being born of a woman is crucial. The nature of His birth shows that human sexuality is good. God made human beings as male and female, and then announced that His creation was "very good" (Gen. 1:31). Jesus took on male human flesh and entered the world through the womb of a woman, confirming the goodness of both male and female sexuality.

Nevertheless, in the Lord woman is not independent of man nor man of woman; for as woman was made from man, so man is now born of woman.

What does this teach us about the role gender plays in God's design for humanity?

In taking on human flesh, born of a woman as a being with a specific sex, Jesus showed that male and female sexuality depend on each another; men and women need each other for their existence. In taking on male flesh *and* being born through a woman, Jesus affirmed the connectedness and importance of male and female sexuality.

READ HEBREWS 4:15.

For we do not have a high priest who is unable to sympathize with our weaknesses, but one who in every respect has been tempted as we are, yet without sin.

How does it give you strength in your struggles to know that Jesus faced the same temptations?

When He became a human being, Jesus came to understand our struggles so He could help us through them. While on earth, Jesus experienced temptation of all kinds. But He endured without sinning. God understands the depths of our temptations and promises to sustain us through them if we humbly ask Him for help and rely on His grace (see 1 Cor. 10:13).

Again, Jesus was not sexually active, but He did experience the world as a human being. His sexuality shaped how He related to His mom, His disciples, and His female followers. This is important because it demonstrates that sexuality goes much deeper than simply "having sex." We tend to reduce sex to the physical act of sexual intercourse, but our sexuality involves so much more. Sexuality refers to how we uniquely understand and experience the world as males and females.

In what ways do we express our sexuality other than sexual activity?

How do you relate differently to the opposite sex?

Reducing sexuality to sex misses a deeper truth about what it means to be human. Whether married or single, sexually active or practicing abstinence, all of us are designed by God as sexual beings. We experience the world through our sexuality.

Now that we understand the difference between sexuality and sexual activity, it's important to explore the purpose of sex, singleness, and marriage.

In Session 2, we examined the difference between "freedom from" and "freedom for." "Freedom from" is having the ability to make choices without constraint. "Freedom for" involves using something according to its purpose.

This also applies to sex.

Why did God give us sex?

According to God—the Creator of sex—there are three primary purposes for sex.

SEX IS FOR PROCREATION.

READ GENESIS 1:28 IN YOUR BIBLE.

What is the first purpose of sex?

It should come as no surprise that sex is about making babies. After creating humans as male and female, God blessed them and said, "Be fruitful and multiply and fill the earth and subdue it" (Gen. 1:28). This is both a blessing and a command from God. Whether a child is the result or not, sex between a man and woman has the ability to and is designed to produce new life.

SEX BRINGS UNITY.

READ GENESIS 2:24 IN YOUR BIBLE.

What is the second purpose of sex?

One of the most powerful aspects of sex is its ability to bond people together, to bring unity. When a couple has sex, something changes in their relationship. They have entered into a deeper unity that is physical, spiritual, emotional, relational, and even biochemical. (The biochemical nature is one reason it is especially difficult for teens to break up after they have been sexually active.) God designed sex to help bond a man and his wife together for life.

SEX FORESHADOWS HEAVEN.

READ EPHESIANS 5:31-32 IN YOUR BIBLE.

What is marriage being compared to in these verses?

How does this explain the spiritual purpose of sex and marriage?

The Bible begins with Adam and Eve uniting their lives together according to God's design (see Gen. 2). In Ephesians, the apostle Paul explains that marriage has existed since creation to point us to the mysterious union between Christ and the church.

As we saw earlier, the "one flesh" union of a man and woman is a bond that includes emotional, relational, spiritual, and physical elements. When people focus only on the physical element, they miss the deeper unity—the intimate connection—that occurs between two people in the act of sex.

Here is something our culture completely misses: even the most wonderful sex life can't satisfy the human heart's craving for love and connection. The sexual union only foreshadows something better in the future. As wonderful as it is, sexual union on earth points to, anticipates, and foreshadows a deeper union we will all experience in heaven.

Knowing this, why do you think Satan is so intent on twisting our understanding of the nature of sex?

If Satan can confuse people about sex, he can confuse them about heaven. But understanding the truth about the purpose of sex and orienting our lives around it sets us free to experience love, sex, and relationships as God designed them.

DAY ONE
TRUE HAPPINESS

From music to movies to social media, sex is everywhere. Since our culture has lost sight of the transcendent meaning of sex, many people today think sex itself is the route to happiness.

Where do you see evidence of this misunderstanding about sex?

Have you ever been tempted to believe it? Why or why not?

This kind of attitude isn't new. In fact, the apostle Paul wrote about this very same issue nearly two thousand years ago.

READ ROMANS 1:18-20.

> *For the wrath of God is revealed from heaven against all ungodliness and unrighteousness of men, who by their unrighteousness suppress the truth. For what can be known about God is plain to them, because God has shown it to them. For his invisible attributes, namely, his eternal power and divine nature, have been clearly perceived, ever since the creation of the world, in the things that have been made. So they are without excuse.*

What does this teach us about God's moral law? How do we know about it?

Describe what this teaches about unbelievers in relation to God's law.

NOW READ ROMANS 1:21-23.

For although they knew God, they did not honor him as God or give thanks to him, but they became futile in their thinking, and their foolish hearts were darkened. Claiming to be wise, they became fools, and exchanged the glory of the immortal God for images resembling mortal man and birds and animals and creeping things.

In these verses, what actions did people take to reject God?

What about our culture? What do people pursue instead of God today?

When have you been tempted to pursue things or people instead of God?

FINALLY, READ ROMANS 1:24-25.

Therefore God gave them up in the lusts of their hearts to impurity, to the dishonoring of their bodies among themselves, because they exchanged the truth about God for a lie and worshiped and served the creature rather than the Creator, who is blessed forever! Amen.

What did God do in response to the people's sin?

What does this teach us about the seriousness of sexual sin?

Just like in Paul's day, rather than worshiping the Creator (of sex), people today worship the created thing (that is, sex itself). The Bible calls this idolatry. Sounds serious, doesn't it? That's because it is. Rejecting God's sexual ethic is a symptom of an even bigger issue within our hearts.

DAY TWO
THREE MYTHS AND THE TRUTH

During this week's group session, we discussed three purposes of sex: procreation, unity, and the anticipation of heaven. Now, let's examine three myths about sex.

MYTH #1: SEX IS NOT A BIG DEAL.

In 2019, Planned Parenthood launched an online chatbot named Roo to answer student questions about sex, pregnancy, and other sexual health issues. One of the questions initially trending on the site was, "What's the right age to have sex for the first time?" [2]

How would you respond to this question?

The answer Roo offers is, "It's all about picking the right age for you, which might be totally different than the right age for other people. It may seem like everybody you know is having sex, but that's definitely not true. The average age when people have sex for the first time is around 17." [2]

How does this compare to your response?

How does it ignore what you've learned regarding God's design for sex?

When I shared this with a group of high school students, a senior observed that Planned Parenthood assumes sex is not a big deal. There is no mention of marriage, commitment, or children. Sex is pictured as an activity entirely dependent on the relative feelings of the individual. They say: If you feel ready, then go for it.

At the heart of the world's perception of sex today is the idea that sex is not a big deal; it's just another recreational activity for consenting teens and adults. This is clearly not God's design.

MYTH #2: SEX IS ONLY A PRIVATE ACT.

One of the most common sayings concerning sex today is that it is a 100 percent private act between two (or more) consenting adults and there should be no criticism or regulation of what consenting adults choose to do behind closed doors.

Do you think sex simply a private act between two consenting adults? Explain.

Name some of the consequences—public and private—of sex.

Sex is not meant to be a public act. It is meant to be experienced with privacy. But it's impossible to separate the private act of sex from its public consequences. Sex may be practiced in private, but it concerns the whole community. Consider these consequences:

- **Sexually transmitted diseases (STDs):** According to the Center for Disease Control (CDC), roughly twenty million new infections of sexually transmitted diseases occur every year in America, and half of these are in young people ages 15–24. The estimated health care costs are $16 billion per year.[3] This is an expense everyone pays for—sexually active or not.
- **Unwanted Pregnancy:** Sex is the natural means by which humans procreate. Since sex has the potential of creating new life—a result that affects the entire community—it can't be limited to the walls of the bedroom. Sex quite literally affects everyone.
- **Character:** Our sexual experiences deeply shape our character. Sex is a big deal, and since our sexual experiences shape the development of our own character, they influence how we treat other people beyond the bedroom.

MYTH #3: "SEX" SIMPLY MEANS SEXUAL INTERCOURSE.

Why does sexual purity need to go beyond only sexual intercourse?

Someone who has never had sexual intercourse is called a virgin. However, sexual purity involves more sexual activity than just intercourse. Sexual purity involves all aspects of our sexuality, from our bodies, to our minds, to our eyes, to even our words.

Sexual activity with someone to whom you're not married will always bring guilt and regret. This is because it's a misuse of God's design for sex. God's design leads to sexual activity that doesn't make you feel guilty and is celebrated by Him. Don't settle for the cheap imitation of uncommitted sexual activity. God wants what is best for you.

DAY THREE
WHATEVER IS PURE

Some time ago, I had a conversation with a young man who told me he was a virgin. But as we continued talking, it became clear he had gone pretty far sexually with a girl, even though they had never had sexual intercourse.

Sadly, this young man had adopted the idea that virtually any sexual behavior was permissible outside of marriage except sexual intercourse. How had he gotten this idea? Clearly not from Scripture.

Genesis 4:1 says that "Adam knew his wife Eve." In Hebrew, the word translated "knew" is *yada*. The word is an common expression for sexual intercourse in the Old Testament,[4] but it carries the idea of a deeper relational union involving the mind, soul, and body.[5] The Jewish understanding is that sex is a holistic activity in which the body cannot be separated from the mind.

READ ROMANS 6:13 (NIV).

Do not offer any part of yourself to sin as an instrument of wickedness, but rather offer yourselves to God as those who have been brought from death to life; and offer every part of yourself to him as an instrument of righteousness.

What activities reflect a life that has been brought from death to life?

According to Romans 6:13, how should Christians use their bodies? In everyday life, what does this look like?

Finally, brothers, whatever is true, whatever is honorable, whatever is just, whatever is pure, whatever is lovely, whatever is commendable, if there is any excellence, if there is anything worthy of praise, think about these things.

What are things you consider to be honorable, just, pure, lovely, commendable, excellent, and worthy of praise?

How do you cultivate such thoughts in your mind?

Which of these things do you find most difficult to think about? Why?

These verses teach us that God wants us to be pure in _____, soul, and _____.

Do you believe it's possible to be thinking about "whatever is pure" or "whatever is lovely" while engaging in any kind of sexual behavior? If we are honest with ourselves, I think we know the answer is no.

God wants each of us to be pure in body, soul, and mind. He is not interested in us doing whatever we want sexually short of having sexual intercourse, but in us loving Him and other people with all that we are.

RELATIONSHIP STATUS

START

Are you under the impression that getting married is the "right" thing to do if you are a Christian? If so, why do you think that is?

According to the Bible, singleness and marriage are equal ways of serving and honoring God. Neither is better or more important than the other. We need both married couples and single people in the church. The apostle Paul even described singleness as a gift for the church (see 1 Cor. 7:7).

Every person is single at some point. If you are an older teen right now and want to get married someday, you will likely be single for at least a few more years to come. If you're a younger teen, then you have more years of waiting ahead of you. That can seem like a long time!

Think specifically about this season of life. What are some unique ways you can honor God while you are single?

WATCH

WATCH THE SESSION 6 VIDEO. FILL IN THE BLANKS AS YOU FOLLOW ALONG.

1. The Bible is very _____—from the beginning through the end—what God's _____ is for sex and marriage.

2. From the beginning, God designed sex to be one _____ and one _____ who become one flesh for one _____.

3. The direction of their _____ was dishonorable and not in line with _____ design.

4. God's design is _____.

5. Ultimately, our contentment is in _____ God and in loving other _____.

6. Whether _____ or _____, we're called to love God and love other people.

DISCUSS

Both singleness and marriage can be beautiful ways of loving God and loving other people. The apostle Paul makes it clear: both are equal gifts for the church.

In 1 Corinthians 7:7, Paul tells Corinthian believers that he wishes they could all be single like him. "But," he says, "each has his own gift from God, one of one kind and one of another." The two gifts Paul discusses here are singleness and marriage. His point is not that some people have the "gift" of singleness—a gift from God to remain content without marriage. Paul emphasizes that both singleness and marriage are important gifts to build up the church. Singleness is good. Marriage is good. Both are valued and necessary to the church.

READ 1 CORINTHIANS 7:32-35.

I want you to be free from anxieties. The unmarried man is anxious about the things of the Lord, how to please the Lord. But the married man is anxious about worldly things, how to please his wife, and his interests are divided. And the unmarried or betrothed woman is anxious about the things of the Lord, how to be holy in body and spirit. But the married woman is anxious about worldly things, how to please her husband. I say this for your own benefit, not to lay any restraint upon you, but to promote good order and to secure your undivided devotion to the Lord.

What are some unique ways an unmarried Christian can serve the Lord?

What are some unique ways a married Christian can serve the Lord?

Singleness and marriage are equal ways of serving the Lord. Both offer unique blessings, and both have unique challenges. Whether single or married, we are each called to find our identity in Christ and to use our marital status in service to the Lord.

Remember, our lives are not our own. We often approach life with the goal of getting the most out of it that we can. But if we focus on living for God, then we don't have to worry about "missing out" on the things of this world.

THE PURPOSE OF SINGLENESS

Although we know single people have equal value with married people in the church, that isn't always the message they receive. For this reason, it's important to remember—even as young, single people—that God has given us all gifts to use to serve Him and others well. Still, serving the Lord as a single person can be difficult, even discouraging. We all need community, encouragement, and support to serve the Lord like He called us to. Married people in God-honoring and healthy marriages have community and a built-in support system. But what about single people in the church?

Here are a few tips to serving the Lord when you're single.

- **Develop healthy relationships.** We need healthy relationships with God and other people.
- **Dig deeper in your faith.** Cultivate the desire to live in obedience to Jesus through the power of the Holy Spirit and spiritual disciplines.
- **Look to Jesus as the example.** Remember, Jesus was completely human. He was tempted in every way like us—including sexual temptation—but He never sinned (see Heb. 4:15). Jesus understands completely what single people go through in their daily temptation.

What are some ways single people can develop healthy relationships with others? How can you start building healthy relationships now?

Share a few ways you can dig deeper in your faith to live in obedience to Jesus.

How does Jesus provide a perfect example for single people to serve God?

Although Jesus experienced sexual temptations, He never touched a woman inappropriately or indulged a single sexual fantasy. He lived the most relationally content life ever.

What does this tell us about the relationship between sexual activity and having a full, meaningful life?

Sexual activity is not necessary for a meaningful and full life. Jesus found meaning through obedience to God and in loving, faithful relationships with family and friends. He was content in His sexuality as a single man even though He abstained from sex. Jesus's life demonstrates something totally counter-cultural: sex is not required for a healthy and thriving life. This was true when Jesus walked the earth, and it's true today.

How can a life be healthy and thriving apart from sexual activity?

The "one-flesh" union points to the ultimate fulfillment all believers will experience with God and others in heaven. Singleness also beautifully foreshadows heaven, although in a different way.

The ultimate destiny for believers is a heavenly state of perfect community. Given that there will be no sin, fear, or shame, we will be able to love God and other people—which is what we were made for—without any limitations. We will no longer be tempted to believe sexual experiences or human relationships alone can bring ultimate contentment.

Single people play the vital role of reminding the church that ultimate satisfaction comes in the resurrection when we will know God fully. They remind us that our ultimate satisfaction is found in marriage, although not marriage to a fellow human being of the opposite sex. It is found in our heavenly marriage (as the church, the bride) to Christ (the groom). (See Eph. 5:32; Rev. 19:6-9.)

THE PURPOSE OF MARRIAGE

What do you think is the purpose of marriage?

God designed marriage to show His love for the church. In the Old Testament, marriage is a metaphor describing God's relationship to Israel (see Jer. 3:14). God did not merely have a legal contract with Israel; He created a loving covenant with them that was shown through marriage. This is why Israel's unfaithfulness to God is often compared to adultery (see Jer. 3:6-8).

In the New Testament, marriage between a husband and wife serves as a picture of Christ and His love for the church. The union of a man and a woman demonstrate the greater union of Christ and His followers.

With this in mind, why is faithfulness in marriage so important?

Unfaithful marriages—especially in the church—distort how people understand Christ's faithful love for the church.

God also designed marriage to show His relational character. While Christians believe in one God, we also believe God exists as three distinct Persons—Father, Son, and Holy Spirit. While there is one God in being, there are three Persons who share the divine nature. As the Father, Son, and Holy Spirit, God is a relational being in His very nature.

How does God's nature as a relational being relate to us and to marriage?

God designed marriage for children to thrive and for the benefit of society. The enemy wants to tear apart the families God has built. Because we live in a sinful and broken world, many kids grow up in homes that look different than what we see prescribed in Scripture. Kids who live in homes with a loving mom and dad who have a healthy relationship are less likely to drop out of school, abuse drugs and alcohol, attempt suicide, or become poor. Children without a mom or dad in the home are at increased risk for health, academic, emotional, and behavioral problems. There are certainly individuals who don't fall into this category, but overall, kids do best in a home with a mom and a dad.[1]

> **How does a home with a mom and dad who love each other follow God's design for marriage and family?**

THE DESIGN FOR RELATIONSHIPS

We've talked about God's design for marriage. What is it?

One _____ + one _____ who become one _____ for one _____

Our culture doesn't agree with God's design for sex and marriage. Most people believe you should be able to love whoever you want to love—even if that happens to be a person of the same gender. But that isn't what God's Word says.

The Bible says God created people to be "male and female" (Gen. 1:27), and He blessed them in their purpose as uniquely created, complimentary human beings (see Gen. 1:22). From the very beginning, God's design has been one man and one woman, who become one flesh, for one lifetime. (See Matt 19:3-5; Rom. 1:26-27.)

We'll dig into this more in the next session, but as we talk about the purpose of marriage, it's important to understand this foundational piece: marriage was designed for the union of a man and a woman, not two people of the same sex.

> **How can you share this message in a loving way to a world who does not believe this to be true?**

Here is the bottom line about marriage. Marriage is not about you and it is not about your spouse. Marriage is about God's kingdom. When you commit your marriage to this greater purpose, and your spouse does too, you experience the beauty and richness of marriage as God designed it.

DAY ONE

MYTHS ABOUT SINGLENESS

Do you think a Christian who remains single can have a full, meaningful life? Why or why not?

List benefits of remaining single.

List challenges of being single.

Let's examine three myths people believe about singleness.

MYTH #1: SINGLENESS MEANS NO FAMILY.

Some of my single friends enjoy singleness and don't want to get married. Others want to be married, but for whatever reason are not. Does this mean they don't have a family?

What do you think? Do single people have a family? Explain.

In the Old Testament, the family was central to God's plan for filling the earth and redeeming it. But Jesus transforms the nature of family in the New Testament.

READ MATTHEW 12:46-50.

While he was still speaking to the people, behold, his mother and his brothers stood outside, asking to speak to him. But he replied to the man who told him, "Who is my mother, and who are my brothers?" And stretching out his hand toward his disciples, he said, "Here are my mother and my brothers! For whoever does the will of my Father in heaven is my brother and sister and mother."

Jesus taught that status is not determined by the natural family (such as mom, dad, brothers, sisters, etc.), but based on a relationship with God. Brothers and sisters in Christ are now more important than brothers and sisters in the natural family.

Single people may not have a spouse or biological children, but they are equal members of God's family right along with married people. We must treat them that way.

MYTH #2: SINGLENESS IS EASY.

For many young people, the single adult life can seem like a thrilling adventure. Go where you want. Eat what you want. Basically, do what you want, when you want to, and however you want to do it. You are the captain of your soul. Right?

How do you tend to view the single life?

But many people find the single life quite challenging. It means no lifetime partnership of a spouse, no sex, and no children. Companionship comes from friendship, but friendships are not always as faithful and committed as a spouse and children.

How can singles find the strength to be faithful? The key is the same for both single people and married people: look to Christ for contentment. Neither singleness nor marriage can bring lasting contentment. The key is not to make singleness or marriage into our source of contentment, but to look to Christ regardless of our relationship status.

MYTH #3: SINGLENESS IS TOO DIFFICULT.

Rather than viewing marriage as too difficult for some to embrace, many people today view singleness as the more difficult road. Singleness is now considered tough (often because of the lack of sexual activity), and marriage is considered easy.

But both marriage and singleness can be difficult. Even though the challenges of marriage and singleness are different, neither one is easy. But they aren't too difficult either. Many young people today prove this with their own lives. Although they are a minority, these young Christians reject the worldly narrative about sex and embrace the radical call of Jesus.

How has this study challenged your thinking about singleness as a Christian?

DAY TWO
THE MARRIAGE DESIGN

The best way to find the purpose of marriage is to go back to God's original design for marriage (as we did for sex). After all, God is the one who invented marriage in the first place. The best way to know what to expect in marriage is to ask the question, "What is marriage for?"

How would you answer the question: What is marriage for?

This takes us back to Genesis—to two vital passages for understanding the purpose of marriage.

READ GENESIS 1:27-28A; 2:24.

> *So God created man in his own image, in the image of God he created him; male and female he created them. And God blessed them. And God said to them, "Be fruitful and multiply and fill the earth and subdue it. . . . Therefore a man shall leave his father and his mother and hold fast to his wife, and they shall become one flesh."*

These passages offer seven important insights about the nature of marriage.

1. **Marriage involves partners of equal value.** Unlike other ancient creation stories, the Bible considers women to have equal value to men. Do you realize how radical this is? The Bible begins with the proclamation that both men and women are equal image-bearers of God. Eve is described as being Adam's helper (*ezer*) but this does not imply inferiority. In fact, God is often described as our *ezer* (see Ps. 30:10). *Ezer* can mean to defend, support, or to be an ally. [2]

2. **Marriage is meant to be permanent.** The man is to leave his father and mother and "hold fast" to his wife (see Gen. 2:24). The Hebrew word for hold (*dabaq*) carries the idea of joining, bonding, and sticking together as one. [3] By the way, the Bible does not need to force this idea of permanence on love. As human beings, we deeply desire permanent love. Think about how many songs are written and sung about a love that is meant to last forever. The desire for permanent love is written on our hearts and described in the early chapters of Genesis.

3. Marriage is a gendered institution. According to Genesis, God designed males and females to complement one another. Men and women share common humanity but differ in their biological gender. Marriage is not an institution of any two people, but of two opposite-sexed people.

4. Marriage is about procreation. As we have seen, God designed sex to be experienced in the context of marriage. A key purpose of marriage is having kids. Marriage is the institution God designed to "multiply and fill the earth" (Gen. 1:28).

5. Marriage is about companionship. Genesis describes the married couple as becoming "one flesh" (Gen. 2:24), which means they become one—spiritually, physically, emotionally, and relationally. Marriage is a complete union that includes a relational dimension. Later stories in Genesis—such as those of Abraham and Sarah, Isaac and Rebekah, and Jacob and Rachel—support the idea that marriage involves deep companionship.

6. Marriage is meant to be monogamous. The man is meant to leave his father and mother and "hold fast to his wife" (Gen. 2:24). When the man leaves his parents' household, he creates a household with his wife. Even though Old Testament figures often had many wives and failed to live this commandment, God's intent from the beginning has been that marriage involves one man and one woman.

7. Marriage is good. As we saw earlier, procreation was not a result of the fall, but part of God's good creation. The same is true for marriage. Although there is much hurt and brokenness in how people experience marriage today, God has deemed marriage "very good" (Gen. 1:31) since the beginning.

> **Which of these seven insights about marriage differs most from how the world sees it? Why?**

> **What are some ways your view of marriage has changed as a result of this study?**

These seven insights are vital for understanding what God originally designed marriage for. If you choose to marry someday, remember that marriage is not about finding your soulmate as the secret to a meaningful life. Marriage is about something much bigger. It is about sacrificing for your spouse and kids and showing God's loving character to the church and the rest of the world.

DAY THREE
A CLEAR DESIGN

READ ROMANS 1:21-27.

For although they knew God, they did not honor him as God or give thanks to him, but they became futile in their thinking, and their foolish hearts were darkened. Claiming to be wise, they became fools, and exchanged the glory of the immortal God for images resembling mortal man and birds and animals and creeping things.

Therefore God gave them up in the lusts of their hearts to impurity, to the dishonoring of their bodies among themselves, because they exchanged the truth about God for a lie and worshiped and served the creature rather than the Creator, who is blessed forever! Amen.

For this reason God gave them up to dishonorable passions. For their women exchanged natural relations for those that are contrary to nature; and the men likewise gave up natural relations with women and were consumed with passion for one another, men committing shameless acts with men and receiving in themselves the due penalty for their error.

What is the connection between worshiping idols and rejecting God's design for sex?

Paul used the term "unnatural" to describe activities that go against God's design for sex. If those things are "unnatural," what is "natural," or abundantly clear and obvious, about God's design for sex?

Paul explained that just as turning to idols violates our rightful duty to worship our Creator, turning to homosexual behavior violates God's natural design for the use of the body as male and female.

How does homosexual behavior worship and serve the creation rather than the Creator?

MISINTERPRETED MEANING

Many advocates for same-sex relationships believe verses 26-27 only refer to sexual abuse of children. Because some also believe certain men or women are born with homosexual desires, they claim that sexual union between those same-sex couples is "natural."[4]

But Paul explained that the opposite is true: sexual relationships between members of the same sex are unnatural—they are not God's intended design (see Lev. 18:22).

As we've talked about throughout the book, God designed marriage for one man and one woman for life. When Paul said "natural," this is what he meant.

Our hearts are imperfect and our desires aren't always good, or as Mark 7:20-22 says, "And he said, 'What comes out of a person is what defiles him. For from within, out of the heart of man, come evil thoughts, sexual immorality, theft, murder, adultery, coveting, wickedness, deceit, sensuality, envy, slander, pride, foolishness.'" This is why following our desires in regard to sex—rather than God's design—is so incredibly destructive.

When have your heart's desires turned out not to be for your good?

Others have claimed that Paul was condemning excessive lust, not loving, same-sex relationships. In this passage, Paul said that people were "consumed with passion for one another" (Rom 1:27). He condemned the shameful acts themselves. But why? Because they reflect a denial of the existence of God by violating His clearly seen design for men and women. (See Rom.1:18-21.)

The focus of Romans 1 is not on excessive lust, but on the idolatrous nature of people who have suppressed their knowledge of God, worshiping things in creation rather than the Creator. And they rejected God's natural design for sexual relations. Paul pointed back to creation as the foundation for sexual morality, just like Jesus did.

Have you put any kind of sexual desire or relationship above God? What changes can you make to put God first in every area of your life?

LGBTQ ISSUES

START

This session will deal with some tough cultural topics: homosexual behavior and transgenderism. Society often sees the church's views as narrow-minded, intolerant, and even hateful. Truthfully, you have probably felt challenged to stay committed to biblical truth and acting in love. As Christians, we must always be committed to both, even if it costs us.

Have you personally experienced conflict with family or friends over sexual or identity issues? If so, how well do you think you handled it?

My hope is that this chapter will equip you to embrace the historic Christian view of sex and marriage and to live out that truth with kindness and grace toward others.

WATCH

WATCH THE SESSION 7 VIDEO. FILL IN THE BLANKS AS YOU FOLLOW ALONG.

1. Transgender refers to a _____ who experiences incongruence between their biological sex and gender identity.

2. Gender dysphoria is the psychological _____ that some transgender people experience.

3. Intersex is a term for people who _____ atypical development of their sexual anatomy and/or sexual chromosomes.

4. Transgender is psychological. Intersex is a physical, biological _____.

5. Transgenderism is an ideology that aims to _____ cultural understandings of sex and gender.

6. The Bible says that God made human beings in _____ _____.

7. The _____ consistently condemns crossing gender boundaries.

8. Scripture gives great _____ to express our biological sex.

9. When we are too _____, we make it easy for people who do not fit these stereotypes to consider identifying as the other gender.

DISCUSS

If you are a Christian who experiences same-sex attraction or gender identity issues, please read these words carefully: God loves you deeply. You are made in His image and He longs to be in relationship with you. Please know that God's grace extends to you—yes, YOU. You are loved. Thank you for trusting me as one voice helping to guide you along your journey of becoming the child of God He wants you to be.

HOMOSEXUAL BEHAVIOR

Some people today push for a "third way" that allows Christians to "agree to disagree" over the morality of homosexual behavior. Wouldn't this make things easier? After all, the Bible allows for Christians to disagree over a host of important issues (see Rom. 14:1-12).

> **What do you think about this? Should the church and the world simply agree to disagree over homosexual behavior? Why or why not?**

The Bible never considers sexual immorality an agree-to-disagree issue. Scripture makes it clear that sexual sin is extremely serious. There are eight places where the New Testament lists activities that God considers sin. As we take a look at some of these lists together, highlight or underline any mention of sexual sin.

READ MARK 7:21-22.

"For from within, out of the heart of man, come evil thoughts, sexual immorality, theft, murder, adultery, coveting, wickedness, deceit, sensuality, envy, slander, pride, foolishness."

READ ROMANS 13:13.

Let us walk properly as in the daytime, not in orgies and drunkenness, not in sexual immorality and sensuality, not in quarreling and jealousy.

READ 1 CORINTHIANS 6:9-10.

Or do you not know that the unrighteous will not inherit the kingdom of God? Do not be deceived: neither the sexually immoral, nor idolaters, nor adulterers, nor men who practice homosexuality, nor thieves, nor the greedy, nor drunkards, nor revilers, nor swindlers will inherit the kingdom of God.

Look over these three lists. What sins are common to all of them?

Each of these lists, as well as the others, contain sexual immorality. In 1 Corinthians 6:9, Paul specifically lists homosexual acts among the kind of sins that prevent people from inheriting the kingdom of God. This is certainly a controversial view today, but if we truly love people, can we soften the inspired teachings of Scripture?

From the beginning, God designed sex to be experienced within the marital union of one man and one woman (see Gen. 1–2). Jesus affirmed this creation account as being God's design for human relationships (see Matt. 19:3-6). Although He did not mention homosexual behavior explicitly, Jesus condemned sexual behavior outside the marriage relationship—which would include homosexual behavior (see Mark 7:21-22).

READ ROMANS 5:8.

But God shows his love for us in that while we were still sinners, Christ died for us.

What does this verse tell you?

How should we apply the truth of Romans 5:8 to people who struggle with same-sex attraction?

You don't need to tell people who struggle with same sex attraction or who claim the identity of being gay that they're living in sin. Instead, aim to love them as God loves us, "while we were still sinners" (Rom. 5:8). While we ultimately hope these friends become believers, whether they do or not, we continue to care. We care about them as friends and as individuals made in the image of God. We should be ready with an answer for our beliefs, and be able to share them with "gentleness and respect" (1 Pet. 3:15) when we have the opportunity.

Some people today will tell you that the Bible approves of same-sex sexual relationships. Others will call you hateful if you embrace God's design for sex and marriage. Don't believe it. True freedom comes from embracing the gospel and living in obedience to Christ, not from rejecting Jesus's teachings. .

GENDER IDENTITY

Now let's move onto another cultural hot topic: gender identity. Our society is undergoing a gender revolution. *Girl. Boy. Woman. Man. Sex. Gender.* To many people today—especially young people—these words no longer mean what they used to mean. The world is seeking to redefine what God has made abundantly clear from creation.

Before we really dive in to this topic, let's review some key terms from this session's video.

What does it mean to be transgender?

What is gender dysphoria?

What is the difference between transgender and gender dysphoria?

What is transgenderism?

"Transgender" refers to a person who experiences incongruence between their biological sex and gender identity. Many transgender people describe their experience as feeling trapped in the wrong body.

"Gender dysphoria" describes the psychological distress that some transgender people experience. While most people with gender dysphoria identify as transgender, some don't, and not all transgender people experience gender dysphoria. Transgender is an identity; gender dysphoria is a psychological condition.

"Intersex" is a term for people who experience atypical development of their sexual anatomy and/or sexual chromosomes.

"Transgenderism" is an ideology that aims to transform cultural understandings of sex and gender. The goal is to uproot the idea that humans are naturally beings with gender and to move society away from being shaped by the gender binary (or the way people are classified into two distinct groups as either male or female).

Ultimately, how you process the transgender question depends on your worldview. From a Christian perspective, there are three important biblical truths to remember.[1]

Truth 1: God made humans in His image as male and female (see Gen. 1:27). So, humans are intrinsically sexed beings.

Truth 2: The Bible consistently condemns crossing gender boundaries (see Deut. 22:5). We are called to love God with our bodies and our souls in the way God created them.

Truth 3: Scripture offers little specificity about what it means to live out one's biological sex. This means that gender expression varies quite a bit across the cultures of the world.

How do you think Christians should respond to gender issues?

Here are three action steps you can take to better love transgender people.

Be motivated by compassion. Gender dysphoria is a deep, painful struggle that often results in tears and anguish. According to one study on transgender teens, 51 percent of transgender boys and 30 percent of transgender girls attempt suicide.[2] This is much higher than the average for teens and young adults aged 15–24, which is 15 percent.[3] My prayer is that God will give you a heart of compassion for this group of people God dearly loves.

Be quick to listen and slow to speak. James, Jesus's brother, said to be "quick to hear, slow to speak" (James. 1:19). Rather than look to "fix" people who are transgender, focus on being a good listener. Ask questions and show sincere interest in their life experiences. Listen. Listen. Listen. Be a good friend.

Speak truth with kindness and compassion. Our culture promotes gender confusion by punishing those who stray from the transgender narrative. But like Jesus's apostles, be more concerned with obeying God than the opinions of humans (see Acts 4:18-20; 5:29). Be bold. Speak truth. But do so with an extra dose of compassion and kindness, knowing that transgender people—as all people—will only experience freedom through embracing God's design for their lives.

What are your main takeaways from this lesson regarding homosexual behavior and transgenderism?

How can we love those who are same-sex attracted or struggle with gender identity or gender dysphoria?

DAY ONE

BE AUTHENTIC

Not all transgender or same-sex-attracted people are pushing an agenda. In fact, many of them just want the same things most people want—happiness, relationships, meaning, freedom, and so on. They want to be able to live authentic lives as they see themselves, whether that's a different gender or as someone who is attracted to the same sex.

They also want to be able to share openly and honestly with you, and you can do the same with them. I know this is a difficult conversation to have—to balance love with not backing down from the truth. But to follow Jesus's example of doing these things, you have to know what God's Word says. Thankfully, the Bible is clear about same-sex relationships.

Let's take a look at four sin lists we didn't cover in the group session.

READ GALATIANS 5:19-21.

Now the works of the flesh are evident: sexual immorality, impurity, sensuality, idolatry, sorcery, enmity, strife, jealousy, fits of anger, rivalries, dissensions, divisions, envy, drunkenness, orgies, and things like these. I warn you, as I warned you before, that those who do such things will not inherit the kingdom of God.

NEXT, READ COLOSSIANS 3:5-9 IN YOUR BIBLE.

NOW READ 1 TIMOTHY 1:9-10.

The law is not laid down for the just but for the lawless and disobedient, for the ungodly and sinners, for the unholy and profane, for those who strike their fathers and mothers, for murderers, the sexually immoral, men who practice homosexuality, enslavers, liars, perjurers, and whatever else is contrary to sound doctrine,

READ REVELATION 21:8.

"But as for the cowardly, the faithless, the detestable, as for murderers, the sexually immoral, sorcerers, idolaters, and all liars, their portion will be in the lake that burns with fire and sulfur, which is the second death."

What does each passage say about those who practice sexual immorality of any kind?

Which of these verses specifies homosexual behaviors? What does it say about those who "practice homosexuality"?

When you talk to someone who is same-sex attracted or transgender, you may be tempted to back off from the truth. But being kind and compassionate or a good friend doesn't mean you have to compromise the truth; you are called to share it God's way.

READ 1 PETER 3:15 IN YOUR BIBLE.

When you sit with a friend who's a part of the LGBTQ community, what do you do?

- **Read, pray, seek.** Read the Bible and know what God says about sexual identity. Pray for wisdom concerning any difficult conversations you might have. And seek advice from other believers such as your parents, youth leader, or pastor.
- **Listen.** Ask questions that show a genuine interest in that person and the struggle they're facing—this in itself shows love and compassion.
- **Once they've shared, maybe ask:** "Can I share with you about what I think it means to be a follower of Jesus? Just as you've been authentic and open with me, I'd like to do the same for you." Then, you may lovingly and kindly express your thoughts.

This doesn't mean every person will react positively or even want to hear what you say, but this is one way to stay rooted in Scripture while also speaking with "gentleness and respect" to those who believe differently (see 1 Pet. 3:15).

There's no real formula for having difficult conversations—these are difficult issues. But, at the end of the day, Christians have to be faithful to Scripture. We are called to reach those who are hurting, including the gay and transgender communities.

Let's be people who love them for the precious people God has made them to be.

Take a minute to think about the truth we've discussed today and throughout this session. What truth could you share if you had the opportunity? How would you say it? Take a few minutes to write your thoughts on a separate piece of paper, expressing what you've learned.

DAY TWO
GOOD FRUIT, BAD FRUIT

Maybe the most powerful emotional argument to affirm same-sex sexual relationships is the claim that historic Christian teaching harms gay people.

In reference to Jesus's teachings about judging a tree by its fruit (see Matt. 7:15-20), some claim the "fruit" of historic biblical teaching is harmful, so the teaching itself must be corrected. Sadly, it is true that LGBTQ people are more likely to be lonely, depressed, and suicidal.[4] Such a reality should break our hearts and motivate us with compassion toward these people God deeply loves.

If someone does not like biblical teaching, does that mean that it must be changed? Why or why not?

What do you think about the claim that not affirming same-sex marriage is unloving and harmful?

There are two problems with the claim that the historic Christian teaching harms gay people. First, there is no evidence that the traditional teaching itself brings harm to gay people.[5] It's my experience, along with many others who work with LGBTQ people, that gay people who choose to go to churches that do not affirm same-sex sexual relations do so because they find meaningful community and biblical teaching. Generally, LGBTQ religious people are actually more—not less—happy than non-religious LGBTQ people.[6] The other problem is that the above use of Matthew 7:15-20 is not scripturally sound.

READ MATTHEW 7:15-20.

"Beware of false prophets, who come to you in sheep's clothing but inwardly are ravenous wolves. You will recognize them by their fruits. Are grapes gathered from thornbushes, or figs from thistles? So, every healthy tree bears good fruit, but the diseased tree bears bad fruit. A healthy tree cannot bear bad fruit, nor can a diseased tree bear good fruit. Every tree that does not bear good fruit is cut down and thrown into the fire. Thus you will recognize them by their fruits."

What is the "fruit" that Jesus talks about?

READ MATTHEW 7:21-27.

"Not everyone who says to me, 'Lord, Lord,' will enter the kingdom of heaven, but the one who does the will of my Father who is in heaven. On that day many will say to me, 'Lord, Lord, did we not prophesy in your name, and cast out demons in your name, and do many mighty works in your name?' And then will I declare to them, 'I never knew you; depart from me, you workers of lawlessness.'

"Everyone then who hears these words of mine and does them will be like a wise man who built his house on the rock. And the rain fell, and the floods came, and the winds blew and beat on that house, but it did not fall, because it had been founded on the rock. And everyone who hears these words of mine and does not do them will be like a foolish man who built his house on the sand. And the rain fell, and the floods came, and the winds blew and beat against that house, and it fell, and great was the fall of it."

What does it mean to build your house on the rock?

Why is denying the teaching of Scripture like building your house on sand?

When Jesus says to judge a tree by its fruit, He doesn't mean we are free to reject teachings that are emotionally difficult to follow. Instead, Jesus means that teaching that leads people toward disobedience and "good fruit" leads toward repentance and obedience. The wise person who builds his or her house on the rock is the one who "hears these words of [Jesus] and does them" (v. 24).

Denying the teaching of Scripture may sound emotionally convincing, but it creates an unstable foundation. We best love God and our neighbors when we are obedient to Christ and when we are faithful to the teachings of the Bible. Doing so builds our house on a firm foundation that does not shift or move, even through the storms of life.

DAY THREE
WHAT'S DIFFERENT?

How can we exercise both grace and truth in a culture conflicted on issues such as gender and identity?

As Christians, we need to be especially careful not to import gender stereotypes into our relationships. When we define gender boxes too rigidly, we make it easy for people who do not perfectly fit the stereotypes to feel like they do not belong.

When I ask Christian audiences who they consider a "manly man" in the Bible, most mention King David.

List all of the characteristics and actions of King David that you can think of.

Which of those do you consider to be "manliest"?

Most will agree that David was acting stereotypically manly when he killed Goliath. But what about when he played a harp or wrote poetry? Scripture offers no hint that these were not manly actions. David was both a warrior and a poet.[7]

Does this mean there are no significant differences between boys and girls? No!

What are some legitimate differences between males and females that are more than just gender stereotypes?

Gender is so important for how children learn. Dr. Leonard Sax notes, "Trying to understand a child without understanding the role of gender in child development is like trying to understand a child's behavior without knowing the child's age."[8] In fact, he considers gender to be more revealing for how a child learns than age.

Consider a few key differences Dr. Sax observes between males and females:

- The average girl has better senses of smell and hearing than the average boy.
- When given paper and crayons, girls tend to draw flowers and trees with lots of colors. Boys are more likely to draw action scenes, such as with monsters and aliens.
- After fighting, boys are more likely to become better friends. With girls, hurt feelings often linger.

Science is revealing significant gender differences that emerge early in childhood development. Failing to recognize these differences significantly harms children.

How does this affect the way you view transgenderism?

What are some practical ways that you—with your unique gifts and abilities—can make a difference in the church and beyond with these difficult cultural issues?

We need young Christians to become pastors who will help people struggling with gender dysphoria. We need young Christians to defend the rights of people who want the freedom to live their lives—and run their businesses—according to their convictions about marriage. We need young Christians with the courage to do quality research that demonstrates the reality of differences in the genders. And we need young people to become communicators who use social media to help advance a Christian worldview in a loving and kind way.

In other words, we need young people to resist destructive ideologies and to take a stand against unbiblical and unscientific ideas about the fundamentals of human nature.

Could this be you?

ABUSE AND PORNOGRAPHY

START

There is a sobering reality today that breaks my heart: your generation is growing up with more access to pornography than any previous generation. More people today regularly watch porn than ever before in history—including men, women, and children.[1] This is totally transforming how people think about sex, love, and relationships.

We need to be especially careful to build our worldview from Scripture rather than the lies that radiate from our culture.

What are your views on pornography? Is it no big deal? If so, why?

If you believe it is a problem, why do you believe this?

WATCH

WATCH THE SESSION 8 VIDEO. FILL IN THE BLANKS AS YOU FOLLOW ALONG.

1. Know that your _____ ultimately comes from being made in the image of God.

2. _____ someone.

3. Experience healing through biblical _____ and _____ relationships.

4. Myth 1: Pornography doesn't affect _____.

5. Myth 2: I will quit _____.

6. Myth 3: I'm not _____ anybody.

7. Jesus _____ you, Jesus restores you, Jesus _____ you, and you can _____ through this.

DISCUSS

Take a minute to consider three of today's biggest myths about pornography.

MYTH #1: "IT DOESN'T AFFECT ME."

Let's see how you've changed as a result of things you've been exposed to.

Have you ever started using a word or phrase your friends say a lot?

Have you watched a horror movie then been afraid to walk through your own house in the dark?

Have you ever hated a song but then started to like it because you heard it over and over again?

Have you ever disliked a food but then acquired a taste for it after others encouraged you to give it another try?

Here's the truth: Every thing we take in makes a mark on our lives because every thought we have changes our brains.[2] Pornography shapes the worldview of those who watch it, and this is especially true for young men and young women. Here is the bottom line: whether you realize it or not, watching pornography unrealistically shapes your expectations, preferences, and practices regarding sex. For example, porn portrays sex outside marriage as exciting, which subtly (but powerfully) encourages you to feel it is okay. Also, watching porn prompts you to accept the false impression that "everyone is doing it." According to a massive study on the impact of Internet pornography on adolescents, young people who view pornography are more likely to:

- be distracted by thoughts of sex.
- engage in sexually permissive behavior.
- sexually harass someone.
- have insecurities about their sexual abilities and body image.
- have clinical symptoms of depression. [3]

MYTH #2: "I WILL QUIT LATER."

Few people realize how deeply porn rewires the brain and shapes human behavior. The younger someone is, the more looking at porn shapes the development of that person's brain, which can have a lifelong impact. Research shows that it is way easier to quit gambling, alcohol addiction, heroin, and cocaine than looking at pornography.[4] Why? Because of what it does to your brain.

How does this truth impact your perception of pornography?

Viewing pornography and being sexually active cause the release of the neurochemical dopamine—the same neurochemical that drives addiction in certain drugs. Like certain drugs, porn also raises the baseline for experiencing pleasure through dopamine. But unlike drugs, the "solution" is not more pornography, but greater variety. This is one reason porn can be so addictive. To get the same "high," porn creates the desire for greater variety each time, which often leads down a more twisted and broken path. Can you see why it is so naïve to assume you can control it? The brain is simply not built that way.

What are some ways this understanding of how the brain functions debunks the myth that people can control their intake of porn?

MYTH #3: "I AM NOT HURTING ANYONE."

This is an ever-increasing belief. But let's think about it.

Who is harmed by pornography? Whether directly or indirectly, think of as many people as you can who might be affected.

Pornography harms performers. Thousands of ex-performers have come forward to share their stories of the dark side of the porn industry. Former female performers tell stories of verbal, physical, and sexual abuse. Former male performers describe the porn industry as involving violence, drugs, and disease.[5]

While you may be tempted to think that looking at porn might spice up a relationship, the opposite is true: marriages suffer when one partner looks at porn. Multiple studies reveal that viewing porn decreases satisfaction, commitment, and faithfulness in a marriage. Spouses who look at porn are taught to think the grass is greener elsewhere, and as a result, destroy the health of their marriage.[6]

Porn harms children. Because their brains are still developing, porn's destructive messages compromise healthy growth.[7] Sadly, there is also a trend of children sexually abusing other children through acting out pornographic sex scenes.[8]

Is there a consequence of viewing pornography that you had never thought of before? If so, what is it?

Given the harm that pornography causes, it's also important to discuss sexual abuse.

How would you define sexual abuse?

According to Dr. Kathryn-Scott Young, "Sexual abuse is one person's misuse of power over another person in a sexual manner."[9] There are different kinds of sexual abuse that range from sexual innuendos (or suggestions), to being forced to watch pornography, to being touched inappropriately (even over one's clothes), to rape. While these actions can often have different effects on a victim, it's vital to realize that abuse is abuse. No matter where it falls on the spectrum, all sexual abuse is harmful and wrong.

What are specific ways that sexual abuse harms people?

Sexual abuse harms people physically. In research for his book *Healing the Wounded Heart*, Dan Allender asked members of a recovery group how past abuse affected their present health. Many were able to identify physical ailments that traced back to their abuse from years earlier. The stress from sexual abuse, says Allender, leaves the body of a survivor "vulnerable, susceptible, and fragile long after the abuse has ended."[10]

Sexual abuse also harms people spiritually. Those who have experienced sexual abuse are more likely to feel lonely, burned out, depressed, and even suicidal. Many abuse survivors find themselves wondering why God could allow such a horrible thing to happen to them, since He is supposed to be loving and all-powerful. These feelings are definitely understandable, to say the least.

What would you say to someone who has been sexually abused?

If you have been sexually abused, please allow me to speak these words from my heart: I am so sorry. My heart breaks for what was done to you. It was not your fault. Please know that many other sexual abuse survivors, including my father, have experienced healing and freedom. I hope this session will be one part of your longer journey to transformation.

If you have not been sexually abused, I pray this session will help you be more educated and compassionate toward those who have been. The problem is very big and very real. With pornography becoming so common, along with the increase of sex trafficking, sexual abuse has become a massive issue today. We must all be ready to respond with love, compassion, and truth.

Why is sexual abuse so difficult to discuss?

What are some reasons victims don't come forward?

The answer is simple, yet powerful: Satan is crafty. Remember, God designed sex to be a beautiful and sensual experience between husband and wife. Sex is part of God's good creation. Satan hates the joyful pleasure of sex, and he is committed to destroying life. He wants sexual abuse survivors to feel too ashamed to share their experiences. While it is more common today for people to open up about their experience with sexual abuse, the church still has a long way to go to overcome the toxic shame many survivors experience. Satan's strategy is simple: spread lies about sex in general—and sexual abuse victims in particular—so they will be silenced and shamed.

How could you help and encourage someone spiritually who has been sexually abused?

If you have been sexually abused, my prayer is that God will bring the right people into your life to help you get the healing you need. When the time is right, I pray that He will equip you to share your story with others so you can see how your life can bring hope out of the darkness you have experienced.

DAY ONE

FILTERS

In the group study, we learned some myths about pornography that cause us to believe it isn't that big of a problem. We also learned some ways pornography harms us and others. Now, let's find ways to prevent ourselves from becoming addicted to pornography.

What are you doing right now to keep from being ensnared by pornography?

Are there any preventative steps you should be taking but aren't? If so, what are they?

Let me suggest a few practical steps to prevent becoming ensnared by pornography.

CREATE FILTERS.

Add a filter on all of your devices. Internet filters easily and naturally build accountability into your life.[11] Ask your parents or guardians for help with this.

READ 2 CORINTHIANS 4:2.

But we have renounced disgraceful, underhanded ways. We refuse to practice cunning or to tamper with God's word, but by the open statement of the truth we would commend ourselves to everyone's conscience in the sight of God.

How can you "renounce disgraceful, underhanded ways" in your life, especially when it comes to pornography?

Who can you rely on to be an accountability partner?

TALK ABOUT IT.

Confess your sins to a fellow Christian and experience God's grace. Burying sin can create a cycle of guilt and shame, but confessing sin brings freedom. Share your struggles with a trusted adult and allow that person to encourage you with God's grace and forgiveness. Simply talking through your temptations and failures—and experiencing love and grace—can help set you free from the temptation of pornography.

What are some reasons people turn to pornography?

Is viewing pornography always about sexual fulfillment? Why or why not?

ADDRESS BROKENNESS.

Understand that porn use is just a symptom of a deeper brokenness. If you have past hurts, they could be fueling your habit. Remember, God designed us to experience healthy relationships with Him and other people. Pornography aims to fill the good desire God has given us with a relational counterfeit. Addressing habitual porn use must begin with the goal of becoming relationally healthy through building intimate connections with God and other people.

And when we are relationally healthy, we become empowered to truly love others.

Which of these steps can you enact right now to avoid becoming trapped in an addiction to pornography?

DAY TWO
THE ROAD TO FREEDOM

Understanding how God views sexual abuse is part of the road to freedom. Let's take a look at some key truths revealed in Scripture.

THE BIBLE IS HONEST ABOUT SEXUAL ABUSE.

What are some instances of sexual abuse recorded in the Bible?

Why do you think these terrible accounts were recorded in God's Word?

The Bible speaks openly and honestly about sexual abuse. Consider these examples:

- In the sad day of Sodom and Gomorrah, Lot offered his daughters to a group of men who wanted to rape his guests. Both cities were destroyed for their wickedness (see Gen. 19).
- King David, who is called "a man after [God's] own heart" (1 Sam. 13:14), used his power as king to have sex with Bathsheba then murdered her husband to hide his guilt. David may have loved the Lord, but he committed a serious act of sexual exploitation against Bathsheba.

The Bible does not hide the reality of sexual abuse, even when its heroes are the abusers.

GOD HAS A HEART FOR THE MARGINALIZED.

While the nation of Israel was expected to care for those who were in need, we see God's heart for the marginalized fully expressed in Jesus. He cared for those with disabilities, the poor, the sick, the demon-possessed, lepers, and others who were considered outcasts.[12]

What does the way Jesus treated the marginalized in His society teach you about the way you should treat people?

Think back to previous sessions. What are some of the reasons Jesus took on human form?

JESUS UNDERSTANDS.

God is not distant from our suffering. Through the person of Jesus, God took on human flesh and experienced the full weight of temptation yet remained sinless (see Heb. 4:15). God knows what it's like to be misunderstood, betrayed, mocked, beaten, and humiliated. He was stripped naked and crucified publicly. While the Bible does not report that Jesus was sexually abused, we can be confident that He empathizes profoundly with the shame that survivors often feel. As one such survivor, Mary DeMuth, explains, "Our beautiful, empathetic Savior understands what it's like to live in this violent, sexually charged world. He knows betrayal and physical pain."[13] If you were sexually abused, Jesus hurts with you.

What does this tell you about any pain you have suffered in life?

What are some ways you can seek to experience healing from past suffering you've endured?

As Christ followers, we need to help those who have suffered from sexual abuse.

We need young Christians to become counselors to help people overcome the crippling effects of sexual abuse. We need young Christians to work with organizations, such as the International Justice Mission, that aim to end worldwide slavery, including sex slavery. We need young Christians to become filmmakers to capture the horror of sexual abuse and tell powerful stories of redemption. We need young Christians to be good listeners to those who have experienced sexual abuse.

Could this be you?

List some actions you can do this week to help prevent sexual abuse or to assist those suffering from sexual abuse.

DAY THREE

DEEPER VALUE

Maybe you have suffered from sexual abuse, or maybe you would like to help someone who has. It's important to look to God's Word for encouragement for those who have experienced sexual abuse.

RECOGNIZE YOUR IDENTITY IN CHRIST.

READ 2 CORINTHIANS 5:17.

Therefore, if anyone is in Christ, he is a new creation. The old has passed away; behold, the new has come.

What does this verse teach you about who you are—no matter what you have experienced in life?

What can reduce your value in God's eyes? What increases your value in God's eyes?

I recently asked my dad how he became a healthy person in light of his experience with sexual abuse. His response caught me off guard: "Son, I chose not to see myself as used goods." In other words, while he couldn't control the evil that was done to him, he could control how he responded. As difficult as it was, he came to embrace the belief that his value overshadowed the abuse. When he became a Christian, he understood more deeply that his value came from his relationship with Christ (see 2 Cor. 5:17).

You are not defined by what happened to you either. God says you are a beautiful, wonderful creation and that He greatly desires to be in relationship with you. Nothing that you do and nothing that happens to you can decrease or increase your value to God. He already does and always will love you to the extreme most.

SHARE YOUR EXPERIENCE WITH SOMEONE.

This can be a scary step, but it is vital for beginning the journey of healing from sexual abuse. People didn't talk about sexual abuse much when my father was younger, but now they do. Teachers, counselors, pastors, and others are ready to believe your story and help you overcome your pain. It's understandable that you would feel fear about sharing your story. But the only way to begin the journey of healing is to open up and share with a trusted adult.

> **Who do you trust that you could you talk with about anything or turn to if you ever needed help?**

SPEAK OUT WITH YOUR STORY.

I hesitate to share this point because I don't want to move too quickly over the hurt and pain of sexual abuse. Dealing with sexual abuse is a journey that often takes a lifetime. Yet many courageous sexual abuse survivors have shared their stories publicly and experienced the power of helping others. My friend Lisa Michelle, for instance, is a survivor of sexual exploitation. Her story is heartbreaking, but it's also a testimony of how God can transform the most broken lives.[14] She is now a speaker and the founder of No Strings Attached Ministries, which reaches out to women who work in the sex industry.

> **How can God transform your past experiences to help others?**

THE
CHALLENGE

START

You may think it's impossible to remain sexually pure in our sex-saturated world—that's understandable. But here's the bottom line: you can do it. Yes, you can follow God's design for sex, love, and relationships starting today.

We can't be perfect. Perfection is an impossible standard and will set us up for discouragement, shame, and failure. But if we lean on the Holy Spirit and focus on trusting God and His grace in our daily struggles—understanding that forgiveness and growth is part of the process—then we can follow God's design for sex, love, and relationships.

What should our daily goals be regarding sexual purity?

What should we tell ourselves when we fall short of God's standard?

I regularly meet teens from around the world who aim to live counter-cultural lives in obedience to Christ. They resist the cultural narrative about sex and trust God to guide their relationships. Is it always easy? No. Do they fall short at times? Yes.

But remember, as we saw in the early part of our study, doing difficult things is meaningful. Nothing worth having comes easy. You can join the movement of young people choosing to live their lives in obedience to Christ.

WATCH

WATCH THE SESSION 9 VIDEO. FILL IN THE BLANKS AS YOU FOLLOW ALONG.

Tip 1: _____ why you're choosing to follow God's plan in the first place.

Tip 2: _____ alcohol and drugs.

Tip 3: Choose your _____ wisely.

Tip 4: Protect your _____.

Tip 5: Rely upon _____ strength, not your _____.

DISCUSS

While resisting temptation can seem overwhelming, the apostle Paul says we *do* have the power to resist.

READ 1 CORINTHIANS 10:13.

No temptation has overtaken you that is not common to man. God is faithful, and he will not let you be tempted beyond your ability, but with the temptation he will also provide the way of escape, that you may be able to endure it.

When we are faced with temptation, what does this tell us about God?

In other words, God is the One—through the power of the Holy Spirit and the love of other Christians—who enables us to live faithfully. You have the God of the universe on your side.

To end our study, let's look at some important questions.

How do I stay sexually pure? Here are five helps for remaining sexually pure.

- Begin by asking God for strength. Rely on the Holy Spirit for His strength rather than relying on your own strength.
- Build convictions about why you are waiting. If necessary, go back through this study and discuss it with others.
- Find a good friend who shares your convictions about sex. Your friends will shape your beliefs and behavior about sex and hold you accountable.
- Be wise about media consumption. Protect your eyes and be careful about the movies, music, and social media you absorb.
- Avoid alcohol and drugs. Alcohol impairs judgment and makes decision-making tougher, which is why it often accompanies sexual activity.

How far is too far? Instead of asking how far you can go, ask yourself how you should treat others with love and honor.

CONSIDER THIS BIBLICAL PRINCIPLE IN PHILIPPIANS 4:8.

Finally, brothers, whatever is true, whatever is honorable, whatever is just, whatever is pure, whatever is lovely, whatever is commendable, if there is any excellence, if there is anything worthy of praise, think about these things.

Can you hold hands with a person and think thoughts that are pure? Sure. Can you hug and think honorable thoughts? Probably. Kissing? Maybe. Sexual touching? No chance. Clearly there is a point of physical contact where thoughts shift from honoring and loving the other to desiring increased wrong sexual contact. That is a clear indication you have gone too far.

Is remaining sexually pure an unrealistic goal today? Why or why not?

Given our sexually infatuated culture, is it difficult to remain sexually pure today? Yes. Can being sexually pure cause you to be treated differently than others? Possibly. But is it unrealistic? No! Many young people today are choosing not to be sexually active. You aren't an animal who acts entirely on instinct. You are a human being, made in the image of God, who is free to love, think, and make moral choices. Anyone who tells you it's unrealistic to wait is lying. Most of all, you have the Holy Spirit living in you and He desires to help you. By God's grace you can choose to remain sexually pure.

What's the big deal with a hookup?

What's the big deal about two people who get together for a sexual encounter without expecting anything further in the relationship? Well, there are often emotional, physical, and spiritual consequences.

- **Emotional:** Since sex binds people together, many people feel used and empty after a hookup: The heart is designed to want more in a relationship.
- **Physical:** Consequences can include STDs and pregnancy.
- **Spiritual:** A hookup involves using someone for your own pleasure rather than truly loving that person.

It's evident that hookups matter and are more than just a casual thing.

Is it okay to date a non-believer?

READ 2 CORINTHIANS 6:14.

Do not be unequally yoked with unbelievers. For what partnership has righteousness with lawlessness? Or what fellowship has light with darkness?

What does this say about dating a non-believer?

While this command is given in the context of not associating with pagan practices, it carries the idea that Christians need to be very careful about connecting themselves too closely with people who have opposite spiritual perspectives. While not all Christians would be good to date, and many non-Christians are caring and respectful, it's unwise to date someone who does not share your deepest faith convictions. Doing so can create a tension between pleasing the person you are dating and honoring God, which is why the Bible says to guard your heart (see Prov. 4:23).

How can I feel forgiven when I sin sexually?

You may feel pain, guilt, and shame from sexual sin. The first step to feeling forgiven is to be sure you have confessed your sins to the Lord and cried out for His mercy. Scripture says that we have all sinned (see Rom. 3:23) but that God will forgive us if we ask (see 1 John 1:9). God desires for us to genuinely turn away from our sin and toward Him. We cannot cheapen His grace and forgiveness by sinning with every intention of doing the same thing over and over again, desiring to dip back into His well of forgiveness. If you have confessed and desire to turn away from your sins, then He forgives you. You are forgiven.

Consider meditating on 1 John 2:1 and Psalm 103:12 and confessing to a trusted leader who can pray with you, encourage you, and help you feel God's forgiveness firsthand.

Let's read those verses together now.

READ 1 JOHN 2:1.

My little children, I am writing these things to you so that you may not sin. But if anyone does sin, we have an advocate with the Father, Jesus Christ the righteous.

NOW READ PSALM 103:12.

As far as the east is from the west, so far does he remove our transgressions from us.

What do these verses tell us about times when we feel like we have done something unforgivable?

Can you be gay and Christian?

This depends on what we mean by "gay." Can a Christian experience same-sex attraction? Of course. Can a Christian commit sexual sin, including homosexual behavior, and be forgiven? Absolutely. Can a person engage in unrepentant same-sex sexual behavior and be a Christian? That's tougher. The Bible is clear that sex is meant for one man and one woman in marriage. It places homosexual behavior (among other things) in the category of sins that keeps someone from inheriting the kingdom of God (see 1 Cor. 6:9-11). While God ultimately judges the heart, practicing homosexual behavior is at odds with God's desire for the Christian life. Ultimately, we cannot claim an identity for ourselves that is contrary to God's design or commands.

Should I use someone's preferred gender pronoun?

Christians are divided on this difficult question. Let's consider both sides. Those who support using preferred pronouns emphasize the importance of the relationship. In the eyes of many people who are transgender, not using their preferred pronoun means you do not truly care about them. So, using a preferred pronoun is being charitable.

People who are opposed to using preferred pronouns emphasize the power of words. Since people can't biologically switch sexes, preferred pronouns affirm a false reality and distort truth. Using a preferred pronoun potentially brings harm to your conscience, the individual, and the wider society. Wrestle through this question with friends and a trusted adult.

Let's finish by reflecting on the last nine sessions.

What is your biggest takeaway from this book?

Which session did you find the most challenging? Why?

Based on everything we've discussed, do you feel confident in your ability to remain sexually pure? If not, reach out to a trusted adult or accountability partner to continue this conversation.

LEADER GUIDE

LEADER TIPS

Thank you for your commitment to loving students well and leading them into a deeper relationship with God and others. The topics we cover in this study aren't easy, and we want you to know you're not alone in this. We pray for you as a leader, that you will courageously teach the truth no matter what students think. We pray that students will grow in their understanding of God's love for them and His design for their relationships and sexuality.

PRAY

Before you meet with your group, pray. Ask God to prepare you to lead this study, and spend time praying specifically for the students in your group before every session. Ask God to prepare students to approach each session's topic with maturity and grace.

PREPARE

Don't wing the group sessions; come to group time prepared. Students will likely have questions, and these are difficult topics. Complete the study and watch the videos yourself before presenting the material to students. Dig in as you preview each session, making notes and marking specific areas of focus for your group. Consider the age, maturity level, and needs of your group before diving into specific topics. Consult with church leadership and parents about any controversial questions that may be covered during group time. If you would like more help with some of these difficult topics, consult Sean McDowell's YouTube channel at youtube.com/@SeanMcDowell.

REACH OUT

Encourage the students in your group to complete each day of personal study following the group sessions. Throughout the week, follow up with group members. Consider reaching out about a specific prayer request or diving further into a question a student may have been afraid to ask in front of the whole group.

EVALUATE AND CHANGE

After each session, think about what went well and what might need to change for you to effectively lead the study. If students seem hesitant to open up, consider placing students into smaller groups as they discuss the video and content together.

SESSION 1 | TRUST GOD

START

This study requires openness and honesty, so take a few minutes to get to know students and help them get to know one another. Laughter is often a good way to help students relax, so challenge them to come up with (or search the internet for) a cheesy Christian pick-up line. (Allow them to work in groups if desired.) After a few minutes, ask each student to share their name and the line they chose or created.

Use the "Start" section on page 9 to help students focus their attention on today's topic: trusting God.

WATCH

Encourage students to follow along with the Session 1 video by filling in the blanks.

Answers: 1) pleasure-centered; 2) yourself, God, people; 3) Father, loves; 4) exist; 5) goodness; 6) good, best; 7) Difficult; 8) wants, us; 9) listen

DISCUSS

Use the Discuss section to guide conversation with your group, digging deeper into what it means to seek God's kingdom first. Here are some key takeaways:

- God's commands aren't about taking away fun, but creating the best space for us to thrive.
- We have a meaningful, higher calling to live for God and serve others rather than ourselves.
- The people we trust influence us the most. It's important to know who we're trusting.
- God—our perfect heavenly Father—is worthy of all our trust.
- Chasing after the world leads to emptiness; chasing after God leads to fulfillment.

Talking Tip: Point out that we might think we know what's good for us or what we want, but God knows what's best.

TOUGH QUESTIONS

This session tackles some difficult topics, such as trust, right and wrong, judgment, and perseverance. Over and over, we see the idea of "Why does it matter?" Here are some questions students might have:

- Why does it matter if we seek God or self first?
- Why does it matter that there is a moral right and wrong?
- Why does it matter that we know how to judge properly?
- Why does it matter whether or not I stay strong in difficult situations?

Talking Tip: Emphasize that God's love for us is the foundation for what matters. As John said, "We love because he first loved us" (1 John 4:19). As we'll discuss in the next session, real love means seeking others' best. So, when students ask why something matters, this is a good starting point. When we know what love really is, we can pursue the things that matter most.

PRAY

- Wrap up by praying for your group. Pray specifically over issues you've touched on this week as you've studied what it means to seek God first.
- Remind students to complete the three days of personal study for Session 1 before the next group session.
- Encourage students to take their time with the questions, even if they don't feel like they have all the right answers.
- Make sure to connect with any students who may have further questions.

SESSION 2 | TRUE FREEDOM

START

Begin by asking students to share what they learned during their Personal Study days of Week 1. Then, use the "Start" section to help students focus their attention on today's topic: true freedom.

WATCH

Encourage students to follow along with the Session 2 video by filling in the blanks.

Answers: 1) right wants; 2) according, design; 3) nature, freedom; 4) God's design; 5) relationships, God, people; 6) free, designed; 7) developing

DISCUSS

Use the Discuss section to guide conversation with your group, digging deeper into what true freedom is. While most people would agree with the idea that freedom is doing whatever you want without restraint, God's Word teaches us differently. Here are key takeaways:

- Boundaries are necessary for true freedom.
- Freedom means living life God's way and cultivating desires that align with His Word and His will.
- We are incapable of living holy lives on our own because sin wrecked humanity. Thankfully, God extends grace to us through His Son, Jesus, and empowers us to live life His way through the Holy Spirit.
- God made us for relationship with Himself and others.

- We find true freedom when we are committed to His purposes and to building loving relationships with others.

Talking Tip: Point out that God's commands aren't about taking away fun but creating the best space for us to thrive, experiencing the rich life Jesus invites us to live. Consider asking students how they've seen this truth at work in their own lives.

TOUGH QUESTIONS

In this session, we consider questions about freedom, purpose, God's will, and the positives of living a Christian sexual ethic. This discussion may bring up questions like these:

- If I'm free, why can't I do whatever I want? God will forgive me.
- What is my purpose in life?
- How do I know what God's will is? Specifically, what about His will for me?
- What's the big deal about following a Christian sexual ethic? Aren't these "rules" a little old-fashioned?
- What does it mean to love God and others with my body and soul?
- Why should I stay committed to a God who doesn't seem to want me to enjoy life?

Talking Tip: Make sure to point out walking away from God doesn't mean walking into freedom. A key question might be: Why is God's radical design for relationships so hard for the world to understand and for us to follow?

PRAY

- Wrap up by praying for your group. Pray specifically over issues you've touched on this week as you've studied what it means to be truly free.
- Remind students to complete the three days of personal study for Session 2 before the next group session.
- Encourage students to take their time with the questions, even if they don't feel like they have all the right answers.
- Make sure to connect with any students who may have further questions.

SESSION 3 | REAL LOVE

START

Begin by asking students to share what they learned during their Personal Study days of Week 2. Then, use the "Start" section to help students focus their attention on today's topic: real love.

WATCH

Encourage students to follow along with the Session 3 video by filling in the blanks.

Answers: 1) Nourish, maturity; 2) protect; 3) Love; 4) best, feel; 5) God; 6) people, best; 7) truth, love; 8) matters

DISCUSS

Use the Discuss section to guide conversation with your group, digging deeper into what real love is. Here are key takeaways:

- Love is more than an emotion. It's an action that involves both body and soul—and a deep concern for others.
- To love means to protect and provide.
- God's commands about reserving sex for marriage protect us physically, emotionally, and spiritually, and they provide true freedom for us in our relationships.
- It's important to balance speaking the truth and doing it in a loving way, rather than wanting to prove a point or show our intelligence.
- The way we dress should honor God and create a loving environment for others.

Talking Tip: A key question to help students learn to ask is: How can I love God and others well today?

TOUGH QUESTIONS

Real love calls students to make some tough decisions, often on issues lacking a specific "how to" in the Bible. Here are some questions students might have:

- What does it really mean to be modest and pure?
- What does it mean to honor God with my body?
- Is what I wear and what I do really a big deal?
- How do I renew my mind?
- How do I speak the truth in love to someone I disagree with?

Talking Tip: Remind students that although the Bible doesn't speak specifically to every single scenario they may face, God does give some general guidelines that can help them figure out the best way forward.

CLOSE

- Wrap up by praying for your group. Pray specifically over issues you've touched on this week as you've studied how to love and honor God and others with your body and soul.
- Remind students to complete the three days of personal study for Session 3 before the next

group session.

- Encourage students to take their time with the questions, even if they don't feel like they have all the right answers.
- Make sure to connect with any students who may have further questions.

SESSION 4 | GOD'S GRACE

START

Begin by asking students to share what they learned during their Personal Study days of Week 3. Then, use the "Start" section to help students focus their attention on today's topic: God's grace.

WATCH

Encourage students to follow along with the Session 4 video by filling in the blanks.

Answers: 1) gospel; 2) fail, needs; 3) judge, understand; 4) God's grace; 5) past

DISCUSS

Use the Discuss section to guide conversation with your group, digging deeper into God's grace and what it means for us. Here are key takeaways:

- Before we can even begin to understand God's design for sex and relationships, we need to understand why we need God's grace and forgiveness.
- Our understanding of our own sin and need for forgiveness greatly influences the way we interact with others.
- Satan's lies infect what God made good, causing us to doubt God's goodness and His desire for our good, too.
- We can't measure God's words by the way we feel—Satan likes to twist God's words. Instead, we need to use God's Word as the measure for our feelings.

Talking Tip: It's important to emphasize to students that no matter what they have done—sexually or otherwise—God's forgiveness is waiting for them.

TOUGH QUESTIONS

This session explores difficult questions about God's grace to us and others and how our understanding of both affects our relationships. Here are examples of questions students may ask:

- What's the big deal about having sex with someone to whom I'm not married if we both consent?
- Isn't the ultimate goal of life to find a good sexual partner and get married?

- Is sexual sin the worst sin? If I've already had sex, will God forgive me?
- How do I get over the guilt and shame I feel because of my sexual sin?

Talking Tip: Encourage students with the truth that God loves and forgives them when they come to Him in repentance—no matter what their sin might be.

CLOSE

- Wrap up by praying for your group. Pray specifically over issues you've touched on this week as you've studied our need for forgiveness and God's answering grace.
- Remind students to complete the three days of personal study for Session 4 before the next group session.
- Encourage students to take their time with the questions, even if they don't feel like they have all the right answers.
- Make sure to connect with any students who may have further questions.

SESSION 5 | GOD'S DESIGN

START

Begin by asking students to share what they learned during their Personal Study days of Week 4. Then, use the "Start" section to help students focus their attention on today's topic: God's design for relationships.

WATCH

Encourage students to follow along with the Session 5 video by filling in the blanks.

Answers: 1) sex, free; 2) earth; 3) man, wife; 4) eternal; 5) cannot; 6) relationship; 7) big deal; 8) private; 9) Marriage

DISCUSS

Use the Discuss section to guide conversation with your group, digging deeper into God's design for relationships. Here are key takeaways:

- All humans are sexual beings, whether they are sexually active or not, and all people were made for relationships whether they're single, dating, or married.
- When God made people in His image, He wove into us the desire for relationship with Him and others. In fact, our purpose is to live in loving relationship with God and others.
- Although Jesus was never sexually active, He was human just like us and tempted just like us (see Heb. 4:15). Jesus had a relationship with God and friendships with others, and He models the best way for us to have healthy, godly relationships.

Talking Tip: Be honest with students about the purpose of sex, how to face temptation, and how pursuing God above all changes everything.

TOUGH QUESTIONS

God created us for relationship with Him and others, but students may struggle to understand what that looks like. Some questions may include:

- What does a good relationship with God have to do with our sexuality?
- Isn't sex the key to being happy? If so, then why does the Bible have so many rules about it?
- Sex isn't really a big deal, though, right?
- Why do I need to care about purity if I'm not having sex?

Talking Tip: Make sure students know that sex is a big deal; God created it as a picture of the unity we will one day experience with Him. This would also be a good time to point back to Session 2, "True Freedom," to discuss the fact that God's commands about sex—when obeyed— allow us to experience truly fulfilling sex in marriage, as it was designed.

CLOSE

- Wrap up by praying for your group. Pray specifically over issues you've touched on this week as you've studied God's design for relationships.
- Remind students to complete the three days of personal study for Session 5 before the next group session.
- Encourage students to take their time with the questions, even if they don't feel like they have all the right answers.
- Make sure to connect with any students who may have further questions.

SESSION 6 | RELATIONSHIP STATUS

START

Begin by asking students to share what they learned during their Personal Study days of Week 5. Then, use the "Start" section to help students focus their attention on today's topics: singleness and marriage.

WATCH

Encourage students to follow along with the Session 6 video by filling in the blanks.

Answers: 1) clear, design; 2) man, woman, lifetime; 3) passion, God's; 4) clear; 5) loving, people; 6) married, single

DISCUSS

Use the Discuss section to guide conversation with your group, digging deeper into what God says about singleness and marriage. Here are key takeaways:

- We can love God and others both as singles and married people; both are gifts that can be used to serve God and the church.
- No matter whether you're single or married, your identity rests in Christ.
- Sex is not required for a fulfilling life.
- You can find meaning in your relationship with God and others, just like Jesus did.
- God designed sex to be one man and one woman who become one flesh for one lifetime.

Talking Tip: Help students focus on the truth—that no matter who or what they don't have, their contentment in life comes from Jesus. Challenge students by asking how Jesus has helped them remain content, whatever their relationship status.

TOUGH QUESTIONS

Culture tells us that a major part of our happiness comes from sex and being in a romantic relationship, but that's not true. Both singleness and marriage come with their own unique struggles. Some questions might arise from the study this week, including:

- If I never get married, does that mean I won't be as valuable in the eyes of God?
- Do singles really have family?
- What's so great about marriage? If I'm single, I can go wherever I want and do whatever I want with no one holding me back.
- Can single people ever really be happy never having sex?
- If I'm in love with someone of the same sex, can I date or marry that person?

Talking Tip: This session begins to discuss some more difficult topics. Take your time previewing the lesson and reading extra resources or reaching out to your pastor if needed. Don't wing it. Answer students' questions truthfully with love and compassion.

CLOSE

- Wrap up by praying for your group. Pray specifically over issues you've touched on this week as you've discussed God's design for singleness and marriage.
- Remind students to complete the three days of personal study for Session 6 before the next group session.
- Encourage students to take their time with the questions, even if they don't feel like they have all the right answers.
- Make sure to connect with any students who may have further questions.

SESSION 7 | LGBTQ ISSUES

START

Begin by asking students to share what they learned during their Personal Study days of Week 6. Then, use the "Start" section to help students focus their attention on today's topics: homosexual behaviors and transgenderism.

WATCH

Encourage students to follow along with the Session 7 video by filling in the blanks.

Answers: 1) person; 2) distress; 3) experience; 4) condition; 5) transform; 6) His image; 7) Bible; 8) freedom; 9) rigid

DISCUSS

Use the Discuss section to guide conversation with your group, digging deeper into difficult conversations about homosexual behavior and gender identity issues. Here are key takeaways:

- Although society may see Christians' view of marriage as outdated, intolerant, or hateful, we have to learn how to balance speaking biblical truth with loving others.
- God loves all people deeply—including those who struggle with same-sex attraction or gender identity issues.
- Sexual immorality is not an agree-to-disagree issue. The Bible is clear that it is a sin.
- All people, including gay and transgender people, only experience true freedom when they embrace God's design for their lives.
- We love God best when we remain faithful and walk in obedience to what the Bible teaches.
- Although there are significant differences between the genders, defining the gender boxes too rigidly can cause some to question their gender identity.

Talking Tip: There may be students who don't fit strongly into their gender stereotype; some girls may enjoy watching football and some boys might really have an eye for interior design. Encourage students that this is okay. Although there are two distinct genders, the definition for what's masculine or feminine isn't always the same across the board—various cultures define these characteristics differently. We are called to embrace the truth that we are gendered beings and that God intentionally designed us as such. However, Scripture allows us freedom in how we express our biological sex.

TOUGH QUESTIONS

The conversation about homosexual behaviors and gender identity issues is a difficult one. The world and the media share a completely perspective on relationships than God's Word, so there is a lot of confusion surrounding same-sex relationships and gender. Here are some of the types of things students may want to know:

- Does God still love me if I struggle with same-sex attraction or gender identity issues?
- What if I don't fit the stereotype for my gender?
- How do I gently and respectfully share my beliefs with people who think differently?
- How can I balance between standing firm in the biblical truth about sexuality and gender and loving others?
- Should I use a preferred gender pronoun for transgender people?

Talking Tip: When it comes to using preferred pronouns, emphasize that this conversation is not about being "right" and the other person being wrong; rather it's about building a relationship with this person that will allow us to love him or her like Jesus.

Acknowledge to students that a friendship with someone who experiences same-sex attraction may not be as easy and straightforward as the one described in the video. If students still have questions, connect them with a trusted pastor or church leader.

CLOSE

- Wrap up by praying for your group. Pray specifically over issues you've touched on this week as you've discussed homosexual behavior and transgenderism.
- Remind students to complete the three days of personal study for Session 7 before the next group session.
- Encourage students to take their time with the questions, even if they don't feel like they have all the right answers.
- Make sure to connect with any students who may have further questions.

SESSION 8 | ABUSE AND PORNOGRAPHY

START

Begin by asking students to share what they learned during their Personal Study days of Week 7. Then, use the "Start" section to help students focus their attention on today's topics: sexual abuse and pornography.

WATCH

Encourage students to follow along with the Session 8 video by filling in the blanks.

Answers: 1) value; 2) Tell; 3) truth, healthy; 4) me; 5) later; 6) hurting; 7) forgives, loves, work

DISCUSS

Use the Discuss section to guide conversation with your group, digging deeper into the damage caused by sexual abuse and pornography, and the healing God can bring. Here are the key takeaways:

- Everything we take in changes us in some way. Porn is even shown to rewire the brain.
- Pornography creates unrealistic expectations about and views of sex.
- Porn harms performers, marriages, and children.
- All sexual abuse is harmful and wrong.

Talking Tips: For students who struggle with pornography addiction, refer to Personal Study day 1. Encourage them to add a filter to their phones; point them toward a trusted adult—like a pastor or counselor—with whom they can talk about their struggles; and help them see ways they can have healthy, God-honoring relationships.

It's also important to know that any person who works with kids or teens on a regular basis is considered a **mandated reporter** (or **mandatory reporter**), and as a leader in youth ministry, this likely includes you. Being a mandated reporter means:

- You are required to report any suspected or known abuse, including sexual abuse.
- You are not responsible for providing proof of abuse, but you must be able to explain why you suspect abuse.
- The exact method of and process for reporting varies by state, but you start by contacting a local authority such as law enforcement or Child Protective Services (CPS). Most states also have a specific number for you to call to report abuse.[1] Sometimes, after communicating directly with an agency, you will also be required to file a written statement.

TOUGH QUESTIONS

The content of this session—addiction to pornography and sexual abuse—may make some students uncomfortable or bring up painful feelings for others. Although they may not ask them in front of the group, be prepared for students to ask questions like:

- If I'm addicted to pornography, how can I break the cycle?
- How can healthy relationships help me heal from pornography addiction and/or abuse?
- I've experienced sexual abuse in the past, and I feel so much guilt and shame. How do I move forward and trust in God's goodness?
- What are some ways I can help those who have been sexually abused?
- What if I am, or someone I know is, being sexually abused right now?

Talking Tip: Be a safe place. Students may not feel comfortable asking some of these questions in front of the group. Don't push them to share for the sake of accountability or support. Create an environment where students feel safe to share, and be prepared for students to talk to you about some of these things outside of group time. You'll have to decide on a case by case basis who to involve, but you may need to talk with the student's parents, a pastor, or a counselor. If the student is more comfortable this way, offer to go with them to show your support.

CLOSE

- Wrap up by praying for your group. Pray specifically over issues you've touched on this week as you've discussed sexual abuse and pornography.
- Remind students to complete the three days of personal study for Session 8 before the next group session.
- Encourage students to take their time with the questions, even if they don't feel like they have all the right answers.
- Make sure to connect with any students who may have further questions.

SESSION 9 | THE CHALLENGE

START

Begin by asking students to share what they learned during their Personal Study days of Week 8. Then, use the "Start" section to help students focus their attention on today's topic: a challenge to live Jesus's sexual ethic.

WATCH

Encourage students to follow along with the Session 9 video by filling in the blanks.

Answers: 1) Remember; 2) Avoid; 3) friends; 4) eyes; 5) God's, own

DISCUSS

Use the Discuss section to guide conversation with your group, digging deeper into what it means to truly live Jesus's sexual ethic. Here are the key takeaways:

- God gives us the strength and a way to escape temptation.
- We can model the way we respond to temptation after Jesus: by using Scripture.
- It is possible to remain sexually pure, even in our over-sexualized culture.
- Romantic relationships with non-believers and hookups are dangerous.
- While it's possible for a Christian to experience same-sex attraction—and God forgives those who engage in homosexual behaviors—practicing homosexual behaviors is at odds with God's design.

Talking Tip: Remember questions students asked along the way and any topics that were particularly meaningful to or difficult for your group. Try to focus most of your time on those areas.

TOUGH QUESTIONS

This session provides answers to some of the tough questions students may have asked throughout the study, plus a few more. Spend some time walking through each question with students, allowing them to ask additional questions as you go.

Talking Tip: It's entirely possible that your group will ask questions that aren't answered in this session. If you don't feel equipped to answer a particular question, that's okay. Be honest with your group, and tell them when you don't know. However, try to direct those students to a trusted adult who can help them.

CLOSE

- Wrap up by praying for your group to remember what they've learned about God's sexual ethic over the last nine sessions.
- As you end your time together, refer to the last three questions in this session. Don't be afraid to share your own answers, as this encourages students to be open and vulnerable as well.
- Since this is the last week your group will meet, and you've been dealing with some heavy topics, consider meeting somewhere new where you can do something fun or relaxing after you complete this group session. Maybe even consider an all-day retreat, starting with study and breakfast in the morning, then going for a hike, to an amusement park, or attending a concert (or bringing in a special music guest) later that day.

TRUE LOVE WAITS COMMITMENT

By the time you have reached this page, you have hopefully gone through all nine sessions of *Chasing Love*. It is my hope and prayer that by this point, the words on this commitment card are an accurate reflection of where your heart is right now in regard to your commitment to Christ in your pursuit of purity.

TRUE LOVE WAITS COMMITMENT

In light of who God is, what Christ has done for me, and who I am in Him, from this day forward I commit myself to Him in the lifelong pursuit of personal holiness. By His grace, I will continually present myself to Him as a living sacrifice, holy and pleasing to God.

SIGNATURE

DATE

NOTES

SOURCES

SESSION 3

1. Nancy R. Pearcey, *Love Thy Body* (Grand Rapids, MI: Baker, 2018), 35-37.

SESSION 4

1. Jeremy Pettit, "The Only Thing Humans Create That Last Forever," *Jeremy Pettit on Communication & Culture*, February 10, 2019, https://jeremypettitt.com/the-only-thing-humans-create-that-lasts-forever.
2. C. S. Lewis, *The Weight of Glory* (HarperOne, 2001), 45-46.

SESSION 5

1. "Ask Roo: The Sexual Health Chatbot from Planned Parenthood," Planned Parenthood, accessed August 12, 2020, https://www.plannedparenthood.org/learn/roo-sexual-health-chatbot; "Planned Parenthood Launches New Sexual Health Chatbot to Meet the Needs of Young People 24/7," January 24, 2019, https://www.plannedparenthood.org/about-us/newsroom/press-releases/planned-parenthood-launches-new-sexual-health-chatbot-to-meet-the-needs-of-young-people-24-7.
2. "Roo: Your Sexual Health Bot," Planned Parenthood, accessed August 12, 2020, https://roo.plannedparenthood.org/chat.
3. "Sexually Transmitted Infections Prevalence, Incidence, and Cost Estimates in the United States," Centers for Disease Control and Prevention, last reviewed January 25, 2021, https://www.cdc.gov/std/statistics/prevalence-2020-at-a-glance.htm.
4. Kenneth A. Mathews, *Genesis 1–11:26*, The New American Commentary, Vol 01A (Nashville, TN: B&H Publishing Group, 2012).
5. Greg Smalley, "Does 'Yada, Yada, Yada' in your Marriage Mean It's 'Blah, Blah, Blah'?", Focus on the Family, March 29, 2017, https://www.focusonthefamily.com/marriage/does-yada-yada-yada-in-your-marriage-mean-its-blah-blah-blah/.

SESSION 6

1. Scott Haltzman, "The Effect of Gender-Based Parental Influences on Raising Children," in *Gender and Parenthood: Biological and Scientific Perspectives*, ed. W. Bradford Wilcox & Kathleen Kovner Kline (New York: Columbia University Press, 2013), 318.
2. Blue Letter Bible, s.v. "Ezer," accessed July 20, 2020, https://www.blueletterbible.org/lang/lexicon/lexicon.cfm?strongs=H5826.
3. Blue Letter Bible, s.v. "Dabaq," accessed July 20, 2020, https://www.blueletterbible.org/lang/lexicon/lexicon.cfm?strongs=H1692.
4. Holman Bible Publishers, *CSB Study Bible* (Nashville: B&H Publishing Group, 2017).

SESSION 7

1. I am deeply indebted to Preston Sprinkle for this section. See Preston Sprinkle, "A Biblical Conversation about Transgender Identities," https://www.centerforfaith.com/resources/pastoral-papers/12-a-biblical-conversation-about-transgender-identities.
2. Russell B. Toomey, Amy K. Syvertsen, and Maura Shramko, "Transgender Adolescent Suicide Behavior," *PEDIATRICS* 142, no. 4 (October 2018): 1, https://doi.org/10.1542/peds.2017-4218.
3. "Suicide Statistics," American Association of Suicide Prevention, May 19, 2023, https://afsp.org/suicide-statistics/.

4. Brad Brenner, "Understanding Anxiety and Depression for LGBTQ People," Anxiety and Depression Association of America, published May 18, 2016, updated October 2020, https://adaa.org/learn-from-us/from-the-experts/blog-posts/consumer/understanding-anxiety-and-depression-lgbtq.

5. Mark Yarhouse & Olya Zaporozhets, *Costly Obedience: What We Can Learn from the Celibate Gay Christian Community* (Grand Rapids, MI: Zondervan, 2019), 29-31.

6. M. N. Barringer and David A. Gay, "Happily Religious: The Surprising Sources of Happiness Among Lesbian, Gay, Bisexual, and Transgender Adults," *Sociological Inquiry* 87, no. 1 (2016): 75-96, https://doi.org/10.1111/soin.12154.

7. Again, my thanks to Preston Sprinkle for this observation.

8. Leonard Sax, *Why Gender Matters: What Parents and Teachers need to Know About the Emerging Science of Sex Differences* (New York, NY: Harmony Books, 2017), 8.

SESSION 8

1. Barna Resources, *The Porn Phenomenon: The Impact of Pornography in the Digital Age* (Ventura, CA: The Barna Group, 2016).

2. Dr. Caroline Leaf, *Switch on Your Brain: The Key to Peak Happiness, Thinking, and Health* (Grand Rapids, MI: Baker Books, 2013).

3. Eric W. Owens, Richard J. Behun, Jill C. Manning, Rory C. Reid, "The Impact of Pornography on Adolescents: A review of the research," *Sexual Addiction & Compulsivity: The Journal of Treatment & Prevention* 19, no. 1-2 (2012): 99-122, https://doi.org/10.1080/10720162.2012.660431.

4. Josh D. McDowell, "The Porn Epidemic: Facts, Stats, & Solutions: Brain," Josh McDowell: A CRU Ministry, updated October 26, 2021, https://s3.amazonaws.com/jmm.us/The+Porn+Epidemic+-+Brain+Chapter+%E 2%80%93+Updated+10.26.2021.pdf: 237; via Gert-Jan Meerkerk, Regina J. J. M. Van Den Eijnden, and Henk F. L. Garretsen, "Predicting compulsive Internet use; it's all about sex!" *CyberPsychology & Behavior* 9, no. 1 (February 23, 2006): 95-103, https://doi.org/10.1089/cpb.2006.9.95.

5. Fight the New Drug, "5 Male Ex-Performers Share What It's Really Like To Do Porn," accessed September 3, 2019, https://fightthenewdrug.org/3-male-porn-stars-share-their-most-disturbing-experiences-doing-porn/.

6. John D. Foubert, *How Pornography Harms* (Bloomington, IN: LifeRich Publishing, 2017), 63-64.

7. Allison Baxter, "How Pornography Harms Children: The Advocates Role," The American Bar Association, May 1, 2014, https://www.americanbar.org/groups/public_interest/child_law/resources/child_law_practiceonline/child_law_practice/vol-33/may-2014/how-pornography-harms-children--the-advocate-s-role/.

8. Barna, *The Porn Phenomenon*, 95.

9. Kathryn Scott-Young, "Sexual Abuse," in *The Popular Encyclopedia of Christian Counseling*, ed. Dr. Tim Clinton and Dr. Ron Hawkins (Eugene, OR: Harvest House, 2011), 303.

10. Dan B. Allender, *Healing the Wounded Heart* (Grand Rapids, MI: Baker, 2016), 61.

11. While there are some wonderful ministries that can help, I personally recommend Covenant Eyes: www.covenanteyes.com.

12. Jonalyn Fincher, "Defending Femininity: Why Jesus is Good News for Women," in *Apologetics for a New Generation*, ed. Sean McDowell (Eugene, OR: Harvest House, 2009), 222-229.

13. Mary DeMuth, *We Too: How the Church Can Respond Redemptively to the Sexual Abuse Crisis* (Eugene, OR: Harvest House: 2019), 46.

14. "Surviving Sexual Abuse and Exploitation (with Lisa Michelle)," an episode of the *Think Biblically Podcast*, co-hosted by Sean McDowell and Scott Rae, January 19, 2019, https://www.biola.edu/blogs/think-biblically/2019/surviving-sexual-abuse-and-exploitation.

LEADER GUIDE

1. "Mandatory Reporters of Child Abuse and Neglect," Child Welfare Information Gateway, accessed August 21, 2020, https://www.childwelfare.gov/pubPDFs/manda.pdf.

Get the most from your study.

Promotional videos and other leader materials available at lifeway.com/chasinglove.

We live in a society that constantly challenges us when it comes to sexuality. Thankfully, God doesn't leave us to find the answers on our own: He shows us His design for sex, relationships, marriage, and gender in His Word. This study will take you through God's Word to answer some of the toughest questions about love, sex, gender, and relationships. We will learn that it is possible to embrace God's design by loving Him and others with both our bodies and our souls. We will learn how we can show love to those who live outside God's design and that God's love heals wounds. His grace frees us from the shame and guilt of past mistakes.

In this nine-session Bible study, Sean McDowell will show you how to think biblically when it comes to love, sex, and gender. He will delve into God's Word to help guide you to know God's heart, desires, and design for our lives and relationships.

Want to watch the *Chasing Love* teaching videos when and where it's most convenient? Introducing the Lifeway On Demand app! From your smartphone to your TV, watching videos from Lifeway has never been easier. Visit lifeway.com/chasinglove or the Lifeway on Demand app to purchase the teaching videos and hear from author Sean McDowell.

For more information about Lifeway Students, visit lifeway.com/students.

ADDITIONAL RESOURCES

CHASING LOVE VIDEO STREAMING BUNDLE
Nine teaching videos from Sean McDowell available at lifeway.com/chasinglove.

CHASING LOVE EBOOK
An eBook format of *Chasing Love*, a nine-session study on God's design for love, sex, gender, and relationships.

Available in the **Lifeway On Demand** app

Stream on these devices: